ENCOUNTERING THE GOSPEL

2024 BEREAN STUDY SERIES

Edited by
BILL BAGENTS

HERITAGE
CHRISTIAN UNIVERSITY
PRESS

Encountering the Gospel

Published by Heritage Christian University

Copyright © 2024 by Bill Bagents

Manufactured in the United States of America

Cataloging-in-Publication Data

Encountering the gospel/ edited by Bill Bagents

p. cm.

Includes scripture index.

ISBN 978-1-956811-55-1 (pbk.) 978-1-956811-56-8 (ebook)

1. Bible. New Testament—Study and teaching. 2. Christian life—Study and teaching I. Bagents, William Ronald, 1956–, editor. II. Title.

2225.007—dc20

Library of Congress Control Number: 2024932406

Cover design by Brad McKinnon and Brittany Vander Maas.

For information:

Heritage Christian University Press

3625 Helton Drive, PO Box HCU, Florence, AL 35630

www.hcu.edu

CONTENTS

Bible Abbreviations   v

Introduction   ix

1. THE SYROPHOENICIAN MOTHER   1
Todd Johnston

2. SHEPHERDS IN THE FIELD   8
Ismael Berlanga

3. THE PARALYTIC   15
Andrew Phillips

4. JESUS, SIMON, AND THE SINFUL
WOMAN   22
Justin Guin

5. THE EMMAUS ROAD   29
Joshua Pappas

6. NICODEMUS   38
Ed Gallagher

7. THE WOMAN AT THE WELL   48
Thomas Tidwell

8. THE ADULTERESS   55
Tim Martin

9. THE MAN BORN BLIND   67
Thomas Tidwell

10. THOMAS   74
Zack Martin

11. PENTECOST   82
Baron Vander Maas

12. THE UNIVERSAL REACH OF
CHRISTIANITY   90
Robert L. Mann

13. THE PHILOSOPHERS OF ATHENS   96
Jeremy Barrier

14. FELIX   103
   Bill Bagents

15. AGRIPPA   110
   Wayne Kilpatrick

Scripture Index   119

Contributors   125

Credits   129

Berean Study Series   131

Coming in 2025   133

Cypress Publications Onesimus Bible Study
Series   135

Heritage Christian University Press   137

BIBLE ABBREVIATIONS

Old Testament

Gen	Genesis
Exod	Exodus
Lev	Leviticus
Num	Numbers
Deut	Deuteronomy
Josh	Joshua
Judg	Judges
Ruth	Ruth
1–2 Sam	1–2 Samuel
1–2 Kgs	1–2 Kings
1–2 Chr	1–2 Chronicles
Ezra	Ezra
Neh	Nehemiah
Esth	Esther
Job	Job
Ps	Psalms
Prov	Proverbs
Eccl	Ecclesiastes
Song	Song of Solomon

Isa	Isaiah
Jer	Jeremiah
Lam	Lamentations
Ezek	Ezekiel
Dan	Daniel
Hos	Hosea
Joel	Joel
Amos	Amos
Obad	Obadiah
Jonah	Jonah
Mic	Micah
Nah	Nahum
Hab	Habakkuk
Zeph	Zephaniah
Hag	Haggai
Zech	Zechariah
Mal	Malachi

New Testament

Matt	Matthew
Mark	Mark
Luke	Luke
John	John
Acts	Acts
Rom	Romans
1–2 Cor	1–2 Corinthians
Gal	Galatians
Eph	Ephesians
Phil	Philippians
Col	Colossians
1–2 Thess	1–2 Thessalonians
1–2 Tim	1–2 Timothy
Titus	Titus
Phlm	Philemon
Heb	Hebrews
Jas	James
1–2 Pet	1–2 Peter
1–2–3 John	1–2–3 John
Jude	Jude
Rev	Revelation

INTRODUCTION

Gospel encounters didn't start with the public ministry of Jesus. Genesis 3:15 offers a prophecy and a promise as God said to the serpent, "He [the offspring of woman] shall bruise your head."

The same is true of Genesis 12:3 where God said to Abram, "And in you all the families of the earth shall be blessed." Galatians 3:8 ensures that we don't miss this connection; God Himself "preached the gospel beforehand to Abraham." The theme continues in Deuteronomy 18:15–22 where Moses prophesied, "The Lord your God will raise up for you a prophet like me from among you ...."

So many Old Testament passages laid the foundation for the face-to-face encounters with Jesus reported in the gospels, none more beautifully than Isaiah 9:6:

> For to us a child is born, to us a son is given; and the government shall be upon his shoulder, and his name shall be called Wonderful Counselor, Mighty God, Everlasting Father, Prince of Peace.

The beauty of this passage stands in stark contrast to the fierceness of Isaiah 53. The coming Messiah—the embodiment of the gospel—would have "no form or majesty that we should look at him, and no beauty that we should desire him" (Isa 53:2). And when encountered,

> He was despised and rejected by men, a man of sorrows and acquainted with grief, and as one from whom men hide their faces, he was despised, and we esteemed him not ... we esteemed him stricken, smitten by God, and afflicted (Isa 53:3–4).

The tragic predictions of Isaiah are reinforced by John 1:11, "He came to his own, and His own people did not receive him." Their ultimate fulfillment came through the horrors of the cross. Some of the gospel encounters explored in this book fall within this sad theme of loss and rejection.

Most happily, the bulk of the encounters explored herein directly intersect John 1:12, "But to all who did receive him, who believed in his name, he gave the right to become children of God." The gospel is the ultimate good news to all who choose faith, hope, and love.

May we offer an interesting reminder? Not every gospel encounter uses the word "gospel." Of course, we need to be careful in terms of translational differences. Some translations prefer "gospel," some "good news," and some use both. More importantly, some gospel encounters use neither. As Paul presented the gospel to Felix, the text reports that he spoke "about faith in Christ Jesus" (Acts 24:24). Paul, quoting Jesus, described his gospel commission to Agrippa

I am sending you to open their eyes, so they may turn from darkness to light, and from the power of Satan to God; that they may receive forgiveness of sins and a place among those who are sanctified by faith in me (Acts 26:18).

Encountering the Gospel takes the broader view of gospel encounters. Any text where people meet Jesus, hear Jesus, or are taught about Jesus qualifies. Jesus embodied the gospel; Jesus is the gospel. He is "the way, the truth, and the life" (John 14:6). He is both THE question and THE answer. Meeting Jesus is the pivotal point—the moment of greatest significance—in every person's life. Encountering the gospel puts life's greatest decision directly before each of us.

ENCOUNTERING THE GOSPEL

THE SYROPHOENICIAN MOTHER

Todd Johnston

FOCUS PASSAGE

Mark 7:24–30

ONE MAIN THING

Jesus has a message of hope and life that is available for all people.

INTRODUCTION

My children love their dogs. The dogs love the children as well. There are many reasons, but one of them is that they know that come dinner time, an excess of crumbs will fall to the floor. Having toddlers, I am not sure we even need to buy dog food anymore. While the dogs would prefer a plate of their own, they are perfectly content with the crumbs. The fact that the children are well-fed from atop the table and the dogs are left with the crumbs that fall indicates their level of privilege. We love our dogs, but we love our children more and they will always have a seat at the table while the dogs are stuck to reside beneath, unseen.

There is an encounter between Jesus and the Syrophoenician mother that references the social positioning of children and dogs. However, Jesus's purpose is to share that those once thought of as the *dogs* of society are just as welcomed at His table as those referred to as children. Jesus is the great King who brings equality to all through a message of hope and life. The interaction in Mark 7:24–30 is a jumping point for Jesus to present this message beyond the borders of the Jewish people. Jesus has a message of hope and life that is available for all people no matter their background. Come as you are, but leave a new creation.

GOING DEEPER

Mark moves at a faster pace than any other gospel, with a focus on sharing the good news message with the Gentiles who previously were thought to be disconnected and without hope to be in God. Mark 7 is a chapter that shares both a message of hope for the Gentiles and a warning for the Jews. At the beginning of the chapter, Jesus is warning the Pharisees and Scribes of their hypocrisy: focus on what comes from within and not what might defile from outside. While this message is about all food being clean, could it also be symbolic? The message of a new kingdom established by Jesus will not be defiled by the Gentiles who enter in with exuberant hope and excitement. Rather, it is being corrupted by the self-righteous hypocrisy of the *leading* Jews from within who seek to run a country club of exclusion instead of a center of redemption for all. Regardless, this lesson is a jumping point for the contrast seen in Jesus's interaction with the Syrophoenician mother.

Jesus's movements are intentional and filled with a flavor of expectation. He escapes to Tyre to rest from what was an emotionally taxing encounter. While He could run, He could never hide. His reputation precedes itself, and He will always be mankind's most wanted. In a land filled with the *dogs* of human existence, He is sought out by a mother of great humility, determination, patience, and faith. Like every good parent, the Syrophoenician mother is desperate for her daughter to be redeemed from an oppressive unclean spirit. Although she had only heard stories, they were powerful enough to convince her of the truth that Jesus was the ONLY solution to her problem. So, she enters the home, falls at His feet, and persistently asks Him to remove the demon from her daughter. This is when controversy occurs.

The woman wanted a miracle, but Jesus would do so much more. Jesus's pronouncement in 7:1–23 that all food is clean would preface the introduction in 7:24–30 that all people are clean.[1] This is the hope the Gentiles were looking for. This is not the first time a non-Jewish woman was helped by a Jewish man in this area (1 Kgs 17:8–24). It was that event between Elijah and the widow of Zarephath that Jesus referenced in Luke 4:25–26 to allude to a time when the mission would turn to the Gentiles.[2] It is no secret that Jesus knew exactly what He was doing when He chose Tyre and Sidon as a place to rest following yet another rejection from His own people.

Verses 26–29 provide an almost playful banter between the Syrophoenician mother and Jesus. Jesus, in a proverbial way, uses three symbolic comparisons in His response. Children are to be interpreted as the Jewish people, bread is His message, and dogs were a common reference for Gentiles at this time.[3] The term *dogs* should not be taken as affectionate in the sense of the domesticated pets many have today. Instead, it is an offensive insult.[4] However, Jesus did not make His statement to be rude and insensitive, but to test the faith of this Gentile mother. It appears that she knew this as she responded with a proverb of her own. Her response was witty and creative, but mostly a faithful understanding that Jesus is for the Jews as much as He is for the Gentiles and all the nations of the world (Gen 22:18). Jesus honors her faithfulness and sends her on her way with more than crumbs—with the bread of life.

APPLICATION

Like all the miracles Jesus performs, this was less about the miracle and more about the message. This whole encounter was a politically stimulated event that set a precedent for Jesus to take His ministry to all people. However, to encounter the whole gospel the reader must be challenged to get practical. In this encounter, the Syrophoenician mother provides us with four practical lessons on humility, determination, patience, and faithfulness.

Humility: I have often found myself in a position of desperation. Being in need typically lends itself to a state of humility. The humility of the Syrophoenician mother perfectly illustrates the posture we should have when we come before the Lord of our lives and Savior of the world. Notice she falls at His feet (Mark 7:25). While this posture is one of grief, it is also one of great humility.[5] It is likely that she heard of Jesus's previous travels to Tyre (Mark 3:8), and she almost certainly understands the negative cultural relationship between Jews and Gentiles. However, cultural expectations do not matter when life is at stake. Jesus provides hope to the hopeless and a message of life to the lost and dying. Our response cannot be entitlement like is often seen from the Jewish people, but humility as displayed by this Gentile. When we come before the Lord and Savior, may we be willing to fall at His feet with humility and reverence, for we are desperate to be found in the saving grace of Jesus Christ.

Determination: The Syrophoenician mother was determined to return home with a daughter free from the unclean spirit. She knew that Jesus had the power to free her from her oppressive state. Verse 27 indicates that the mother persistently begged Jesus to rid her daughter of the demon. This persistence and determination are an example of what our lives should reflect about our relationship with Jesus. Whether it be in prayer, meditation, devotion to scripture, worship, or helping orphans and widows (Jas 1:27) just as Jesus does here, we should show determination in following Jesus.

Patience: Patience is a virtue that our world seems to lack. We tend to want things immediately, and if we must wait, we typically give up and move on. No one can fault the Syrophoenician mother for wanting an immediate answer to her question. However, when Jesus provides a parable instead of an answer the mother remains patient and plays along. While good things might come to those who wait, the best things come from Jesus. So, she waits patiently even after being referred to as a *dog*. Even in the fast-paced world we live in, patience can serve us well. The Syrophoenician mother demonstrates how to be patient with time and people. Not everything will occur immediately, and people will not always respond the way we want them to. Nevertheless, when we remain patient, we will reap the rewards of a harvest filled with love, joy, and peace just as is seen in this encounter.

Faith: It is likely that the Syrophoenician mother has lived her entire life being rejected by the Jews. So, why would she go to *their* Messiah for help? The answer is simple: she had impeccable and unshakable faith that *their* Messiah was also her Messiah. Her response to Jesus in verse 28 shows that she knew and anticipated that Jesus's message would eventually fall to the Gentile people. What is even more remarkable is that she would have been satisfied with just the crumbs. In the end, all she wanted was what Jesus was offering. It was her faith that ultimately prompted the healing response from Jesus. We would do so well to have a faith like hers. When we realize that he is all we want, our lives will be transformed. It will be our faith that will ultimately prompt the healing response we so desperately need from Jesus.

CONCLUSION

When we encounter the gospel, we realize that Jesus takes the unlikeliest people from the unlikeliest places to share the unlikeliest stories of hope and life. It is this hope and life that we now have access to through Him. The story of the Syrophoenician mother not only turns heads and unhinges expectations of the mission of Jesus, but it begins the fulfillment of a promise made to Abraham long ago (Gen 12:1–3). Jesus is for all people (Gal 3:28). So, we respond just as this mother does, with humility, determination, patience, and faithfulness. When we do, we will not only receive the crumbs fallen from the table but the whole bread of life!

DISCUSSION QUESTIONS

1. What does it say about Jesus that He is willing to help those in need even when He is seeking rest?
2. What are the connections between this account in Mark 7 and the promises made to Abraham in Genesis 12 and 22?
3. What other parables or accounts in the gospels are like the posture, persistence, and desperation of this woman towards Jesus?
4. What are the similarities and differences between this account and 1 Kings 17:8–24?
5. Discuss the gratitude shown by the Syrophoenician mother throughout this account.

ENDNOTES

[1] James A. Brooks, *Mark*, The New American Commentary 23 (Nashville: Broadman & Holman Publishers, 1991).

[2] Alan R. Cole, *Mark: An Introduction and Commentary*, Tyndale New Testament Commentaries 2 (Downers Grove, IL: InterVarsity Press, 1989).

[3] Cole, *Mark*.

[4] N.T. Wright, *Mark for Everyone,* (Louisville: Westminster John Knox Press, 2001).

[5] Brooks, *Mark*.

2

SHEPHERDS IN THE FIELD

Ismael Berlanga

FOCUS PASSAGE

Luke 2:8–20

ONE MAIN THING

As a believer, your story is powerful because it has been merged with God's story of redemption. Each generation within our spiritual lineage added a unique strand to the grand story of redemption. Tell your gospel-encountered story!

INTRODUCTION

Luke 2:8–20 contains multi-layered glimpses into how God transformed the world and brought salvation. In this offering, we are going to explore one layer in particular. We are going to look at how God modeled the spread of the gospel through this divine interaction with the shepherds.

Ultimately, the sharing of one's gospel-encountered

story was to be the primary means of reaching the lost in the age of the Kingdom of God! As Paul described it in Romans 1:16–17, the power of the gospel to save and to reveal the righteousness of God was to be transmitted from faith unto faith or disciples making disciples through the sharing of the good news (Rom 15:14–15). The fact that you are reading this today means that *God's divine model for* spreading *the* good news was a success! In our passage, *we are going to look at* how the good news *moved* from a proclamation to an invitation, then a merging, and finally to a retelling. Let us explore these ideas further.

THE PROCLAMATION

The proclamation of the good news by the messengers to the shepherds began with the great sign of the glory of the Lord. What a powerful statement that was made here. I invite you to read the glory of God as a symbol of His presence. Once sin entered the world, the presence of God could not abide with mankind as it had in the Garden of Eden. Incrementally, the Lord restored His presence starting with the Tabernacle (Exod 40:34). Eventually it moved from the temporary structure of the Tabernacle to the permanent fixture of a Temple (2 Chron 7:1–3). God's presence was moving. Eventually, all mankind would have access to His presence through the new spiritual temple of God (1 Cor 3:16–17). The blessing of access to His presence would be a blessing made possible through Jesus the Christ (Eph 2:14–22).

The glory of the Lord affirmed the importance of the unique message that the shepherds received. Now that the shepherds had encountered the gospel, they were ready for an invitation to act on what they heard.

THE INVITATION

As if it needed it, God's redemptive message included a series of verifiable facts to vet the proclamation. This part of the proclamation implied an invitation for the shepherds to choose what they would do with what they heard. The shepherds were invited to seek out the child born in the city of David, wrapped in strips of cloth, and lying in a feeding trough (Luke 2:12). I want to encourage you to read the deeper invitation that the shepherds received. By acting on what they heard through obedience, the shepherds were also invited into God's story of redemption. The shepherds now had a choice to make. Would they disregard what they just experienced, or would they act on it? We know from what happened next that they chose God—and in so doing, their stories were now merging with God's story of redemption!

THE MERGING

Our unique human experiences form our personal stories. A unique aspect of encountering the gospel is that, just like the shepherds, our stories merge with God's story of redemption when we act on what we hear in obedience to God. Being a witness to the glory of God and His messengers, invited to confirm and proclaim the message they received as though one of the prophets of old, and finally, they were to meet the Immanuel prophesied by Isaiah! This moment would forever be merged into the retelling of their story.

THE RETELLING

What did the shepherds say when they located the family? Luke records that they "repeated what they had been told about this child."

Their retelling included the proclamation that they received regarding the new age of peace through the birth of the Christ, but it certainly would have also involved how they went from the field to Bethlehem because that is part of what they were invited to confirm. The redemption story as told by the shepherds contained an important new component: their gospel-informed actions which followed the invitation. This is an important point because what God was modeling for them was that this retelling includes not just truths, but the unique ways that humanity experiences the truth. When we tell others about what God has done for us, it is as though we are initiating another proclamation and invitation.

I love that the text tells us that Mary "continued to treasure all these things in her heart and to ponder them" (Luke 2:19). What she just experienced, coupled with her own miraculous experience of God, all merged in her heart to form a new depth to her story.

GOING DEEPER

All believers have their unique story to tell. We each had our moment when we, like the shepherds in the field, saw a great light. I love the way the Apostle Paul captures this language in 2 Corinthians 4:6. He tells the Corinthian believers, the same God who said, let there be light, also "shone in our hearts to give the light of the knowledge of the glory of God in the face of Jesus Christ" (2 Cor 4:6).

When we merged with God's redemptive power, we became a new creation in Christ (2 Cor 5:17). In Jesus and through the merging of our stories with the gospel, we are reconciled with the glory or presence of the Lord. This is the central theme of God's story of redemption!

When we encounter the great story of redemption, we become a part of it, and our new creation life yields new spiritual fruit that gives evidence of that merging! Our merged stories become what Paul calls a living letter, to be read by all (2 Cor 3:2). Allowing others to read our lives is easier said than done. After all, this is a vulnerable act. Stories are complicated, but that's how we connect, process information, and relate to others. Our stories are messy, but our God is greater and He is the God of redemption. He gives meaning and purpose to the hard parts of our story when our stories are joined with His.

APPLICATION

If there's one lesson that we can learn from what God modeled for us in this passage, it is that our gospel-encountered stories must be shared. Someone proclaimed the message to us. We accepted the invitation. We obeyed the gospel and merged it with the story of redemption. We must now decide whether we will retell our unique redemption story to another. Psalm 145:1–7 declares,

> I will extol you, my God and King, and bless your name forever and ever. Every day I will bless you and praise your name forever and ever. Great is the LORD, and greatly to be praised, and his greatness is unsearchable. One generation shall commend your works to another, and shall declare your mighty acts. On the glorious

splendor of your majesty, and on your wondrous works, I will meditate. They shall speak of your abundant goodness and shall sing aloud of your righteousness.

The story of redemption presented in the Scriptures, just like our own, is not one-sided. Life is messy, but God is faithful and just to forgive (1 John 1:9), and He gives strong support to those who are in need (2 Chron 16:9). The world needs to hear the parts of our lives that are difficult because these are the moments that especially capture God's faithfulness. As Paul said, God "comforts us in all our affliction, so that we may be able to comfort those who are in any affliction, with the comfort with which we ourselves are comforted by God" (2 Cor 1:4). A little comfort through a story shared at the right moment can go a long way in bringing healing to our relationships.

CONCLUSION

Today, as you reflect on the incredible journey that God's story of redemption has taken and how your spiritual lineage brought that message to you, I encourage you to think of how you will keep that rich lineage going. Declare the mighty ways that God sustained you and how He has given your life meaning and purpose. Declare these wondrous acts through the retelling of your story!

DISCUSSION QUESTIONS

1. Who proclaimed the gospel message to you and how far back can you trace the spiritual lineage of that story?

2. What was your invitation like?
3. When God's redemptive work such as salvation, justification, and sanctification impacts our lives, our stories become merged. What would it be like to vocalize that story to another?

3

THE PARALYTIC

Andrew Phillips

FOCUS PASSAGE

Luke 5:17–26 (New American Standard Bible)

> One day He was teaching; and there were some Pharisees
> and teachers of the law sitting there, who had come from
> every village of Galilee and Judea and from Jerusalem;
> and the power of the Lord was present for Him to
> perform healing. And some men were carrying on a bed a
> man who was paralyzed; and they were trying to bring
> him in and to set him down in front of Him. But not
> finding any way to bring him in because of the crowd,
> they went up on the roof and let him down through the
> tiles with his stretcher, into the middle of the crowd, in
> front of Jesus. Seeing their faith, He said, "Friend, your
> sins are forgiven you." The scribes and the Pharisees
> began to reason, saying, "Who is this man who speaks
> blasphemies? Who can forgive sins, but God alone?" But
> Jesus, aware of their reasonings, answered and said to
> them, "Why are you reasoning in your hearts? Which is

easier, to say, 'Your sins have been forgiven you,' or to say, 'Get up and walk'? But, so that you may know that the Son of Man has authority on earth to forgive sins,"—He said to the paralytic—"I say to you, get up, and pick up your stretcher and go home." Immediately he got up before them, and picked up what he had been lying on, and went home glorifying God. They were all struck with astonishment and began glorifying God; and they were filled with fear, saying, "We have seen remarkable things today."

ONE MAIN THING

In His ministry, Jesus showed His authority, including authority to forgive sins. Forgiveness is found only in Christ.

INTRODUCTION

What would motivate you to fight through crowds? When I was in elementary school, I distinctly remember my father taking my sister and me to the mall on a Saturday afternoon so that we could spend over two hours waiting in line to meet someone I was excited to see in person... Leonardo, the leader of the Ninja Turtles. That year, the Ninja Turtles were some of the most popular characters around, and we spent most of the afternoon standing in line just to get a picture with one (or more accurately, with someone in a Ninja Turtles costume). Since becoming a father myself, I have thought about that moment often. My wife and I have braved crowded streets and long lines so that our children could see parades, enjoy rides at theme parks, and even meet some of their own favorite costumed characters. We don't mind waiting for people we love.

Not only did my parents wait in lines to allow me to do things I wanted to do, they also spent time waiting for me to get what I needed, however long the wait. Doctors' offices, emergency rooms, waiting areas—when a parent has a child in need of physical help, there is no packed room or long line that would keep them from getting that child what he or she needs. That is what we do for those we care about, and that kind of dedication is present in Luke 5. Several friends of a man who was paralyzed heard there was someone in Capernaum who could heal the sick, and they were willing to wade through a sea of people to get their friend what he needed. This is more than just standing in line for someone they would like to meet; it was the desperation of doing whatever it takes to help a loved one. In doing so, they also discovered Jesus could give what was needed most.

GOING DEEPER

One chapter earlier, Luke described Jesus's ministry in Capernaum. Jesus taught the people there in the synagogue, and they were amazed by the authority of His teaching (Luke 4:32). He cast a demon out of a possessed man, and they were amazed that Jesus had authority over unclean spirits (Luke 4:36). In Luke 5, Jesus displays another aspect of His authority which astonished the crowd (Luke 4:26): authority to forgive sins.

The narrow streets of Capernaum would have been packed with people, many of whom were there to seek healing. Even today, walking through the site of ancient Capernaum reminds us of how small and packed together the homes would have been; there was simply not enough room for everyone. This prompted a group of friends to get creative and head for the roof. Rather than thinking of a typical slanted roof in a suburban neighborhood, picture the flat roof of a first-century home. These were often used as extra rooms for residents, such as when Peter prayed on the roof of Simon the tanner's house (Acts 10:9). There would likely have been an outdoor staircase or a ladder for these friends to access the roof,[1] and they began the work of removing roof tiles. Mark's account tells us they "dug an opening" (Mark 2:4) before they lowered him down on a mat. These details illustrate the faith and determination of these individuals.[2]

Imagine being packed shoulder to shoulder in a small room, craning your neck to see Jesus teach, when suddenly, a hole begins to form in the roof. Your eyes look up to see a paralyzed man, who in many ways would have lived on the outer fringes of society, now being lowered right in the middle of everyone. Jesus not only saw the man in need of healing, He also saw the friends who had gone to dramatic lengths to help him. Jesus noticed *their* faith, which indicates the paralyzed man, as well as his companions (Luke 5:20). Not only did He heal this man which would have been consistent with what He had done so far, He forgave him.

Luke reveals the thoughts racing through the minds of the Pharisees; healing was one thing, but claiming to speak for God, the only One who can forgive sins? That was blasphemy. As Jesus explains, the statement "Your sins are forgiven" is not blasphemous when it comes from the authoritative voice of God's Son. Verse 24 is the first reference in Luke to the "Son of Man," a messianic title Jesus uses to describe Himself several times in scripture (Matt

8:20, Matt 26:64, John 12:23, for example). We find this phrase in Daniel 7, where one "like the Son of Man" was given dominion over everyone on earth, through an everlasting kingdom (Daniel 7:13–14). Jesus had authority to speak divine words, to heal the sick, and even to forgive sins, because of His identity as God's Son.

APPLICATION

Luke 5 reminds us there is only one voice who speaks with ultimate authority. This is one reason the Pharisees were concerned with Jesus; they were accustomed to being the ones people listened to when it came to spiritual matters. His following threatened their power. In a similar way, the teaching of Jesus causes us to reconsider who we're empowering in our own lives. Am I letting the voices of other people, even if they are my friends, determine what I believe? Do I rely only on my own intuition or upbringing to address life's challenges? Or am I willing to let God speak with authority?

Our world today is filled with voices. TV, radio, podcasts, viral videos, social media—there are people everywhere crying out for attention, dispensing advice, and giving instructions. Everyone seems to have an opinion on what we should think about current events and what products we should buy. This is why it is vitally important to carve out time to spend in God's Word each day. There are times when we might be tempted to treat Bible reading like a mundane task, but in reality, it is an essential practice for us to make sure we are listening to God's direction. In a culture full of competing voices, our guidance should come from the true authority.

CONCLUSION

When it comes to helping a person we love, we will go to any extent to help. In this passage, Jesus reminds us of the most glaring need all of us have—forgiveness. Have I addressed my own need for forgiveness from God? Do I feel the same pressing need for forgiveness that these individuals felt for their friends' physical healing? Am I willing to make sacrifices to help my loved ones see Jesus? These are important questions. Forgiveness is only found in Christ, and the best thing I could do for people I love is to share that news with them.

DISCUSSION QUESTIONS

1. Several passages of scripture remind us that every sin is ultimately committed against God (Gen 39:9, Ps 51:4), which is why ultimate forgiveness can only come from Him. How does it change our perspective on sin to remind ourselves that sin doesn't just affect our relationship with others, but our relationship with God?

2. This man and his friends were desperate to get to Jesus. What are some things or events that people in our culture are eager to be part of and see for themselves? How can we point people to Jesus and encourage a desire for them to know God?

3. This is a powerful miracle that proved Jesus's divine identity. Think of a few other miracles

Jesus performed. How do they highlight Jesus's identity as the Son of God?

4. Read Daniel 6:9–14 and reflect on the title "Son of Man." After that, read Matt 26:64–68. Why did Jesus's describing Himself this way receive such a strong reaction from the Jewish religious leaders?

ENDNOTES

[1] Shmuel Safrai, M. Stern, David Flusser, and W.C. van Unnik. *The Jewish People in the First Century*, 2 (Leiden, The Netherlands: Brill, 1988).

[2] Darrell L. Bock, *Luke* 2 Baker Exegetical Commentary on the New Testament (Grand Rapids: Baker Academic, 1996), 373.

4

JESUS, SIMON, AND THE SINFUL WOMAN

Justin Guin

FOCUS PASSAGE

Luke 7:36–50

ONE MAIN THING

Understanding your need for Christ motivates you to submit to and serve Christ.

INTRODUCTION

Luke is referred to as "the gospel for the outcast." His gospel and subsequent history focus on Jesus bringing salvation for all people and taking the message of good news to the "ends of the earth" (Acts 1:8). Shortly after Luke records Jesus's birth, he recounts several witnesses who identify Christ as the "Savior of the world." An angel of the Lord declared to the shepherds that the descendant of David was here to save mankind from their sins (Luke 2:11). Through the Holy Spirit, Simeon proclaimed that

Jesus brought salvation for Jews and Gentiles alike. An aged woman named Anna declared that redemption had come to Israel through Jesus (Luke 2:38). Repeatedly in Luke's volumes, the gospel is preached, and souls are saved, especially those socially maligned. Often, you will find Jesus ministering to "tax collectors and sinners" (Luke 15:1) to the chagrin of the religious elite.

In Luke 7:36–50, Jesus encounters a young woman while He dines at a Pharisee's home. This theme is repeated—a meal at a Pharisee's house is interrupted by a "woman of the city," and Christ forgives her sins. The contrast between the sinful woman and Simon could not be more apparent. You have a man named Simon identified as a Pharisee four times (vv. 36–37, 39). He would have been of the upper echelon of society who seemingly respected Jesus but did not revere him. Then, you have the woman who understood her need for salvation and worship, and who wept at Jesus's presence. She is described as a "sinner" or in need of forgiveness three times (vv. 37, 39, 49). The scene and accompanying parable remind you of an important lesson. When you understand your need for Jesus, you are motivated to submit to and serve Him.

GOING DEEPER

Luke 7 records Jesus violating several social taboos to reach out to those marginalized culturally (7:1–10), financially (7:11–17), religiously (7:18–35), and, in our text, morally (7:36–50).[1] In Luke 7:36, the text states a Pharisee invited Jesus to dine with him. The invitation to dine was common and demonstrated that the man respected Jesus. Often, rabbis were invited to a meal if they had previously

taught in the local synagogue. This man invited Jesus
because of His reputation as a prophet (7:39).[2]

While eating with the group, a "woman of the city,
who was a sinner" (ESV) came to Jesus and performed an
extraordinary task. Her problem was not ceremonial
uncleanness but loose morality that earned her reputation
as a "sinner." Married women were expected to cover their
heads in banquets like this one. To appear in public with
your hair unbound or uncovered was shameful and even
grounds for divorce.[3] Uninvited guests were allowed to
attend and listen to the discussion along the outside walls
of the room.[4] However, intervening would have been
unthinkable, especially by someone of her social rank. She
brought an alabaster flask of expensive ointment. Edwards
suggests this flask might have been from an inheritance.
The fact that she came to Jesus with unbound hair and her
reputation seems to point to the fact that she was not
married.[5] She began to pour the ointment on Jesus's feet
and wash His feet with her tears and hair. Such a posture
of humility, service, and honor would have shocked those
in attendance. She did not care. The woman used what she
had available to serve and honor the Lord. Note Simon's
response of dismay, "If this man were a prophet, he would
have known who and what sort of woman this was who is
touching him" (7:39). Indeed, Jesus was a prophet, and
thus, He told the accompanying parable.

In Luke 7:40–43, Jesus began to teach Simon and his
guests a parable illustrating the significance of what the
woman did for Jesus. He knew Simon's thoughts and
addressed his error before Simon said a word (cf. John
2:24–25). In the story, two men are forgiven large debts.
One man is forgiven five hundred denarii and another fifty.
A denarius was one day's wage, so both men owed signifi-

cant amounts of money. No doubt both men were grateful for having their slates wiped clean. Thus, Jesus asked, "Now which of them will love him more?" (v. 42). Simon replied logically, the one with the more considerable debt. As Jesus began to explain its application, He shamed His host. Simon had not demonstrated even basic hospitality to Christ, dishonoring him before the dinner party. However, knowing who Jesus is, the woman could not help but honor and serve Jesus. Then Jesus drove His point home, "Therefore I tell you, her sins, which are many, are forgiven—for she loved much. But he who is forgiven little, loves little" (Luke 7:47). When you understand your need for Jesus, then you cannot help but submit, serve, and worship Him. That day, the woman left Jesus, being forgiven of her sins and experiencing a peace she never knew before this encounter with the Lord (vv. 48–50).

APPLICATION

There is much we can learn from this scene in Luke's gospel. *First, we need to be aware of the damning effects of spiritual blindness.* Simon did not see his need for Christ. He had some respect for Jesus, given that he invited Him to a meal in his home. Luke 7:39 states he held Jesus to be a prophet. But, he did not see his need for the salvation that Jesus had to offer him. Instead, he saw a man who could not be who he thought He was because He interacted with a sinful woman. He allowed the circumstances to keep him from seeing who Jesus was—the Savior of the world. Do we react the same way towards Christ? Our adversary and his sinful works can prevent us from seeing the illuminating effects of the gospel (2 Cor 4:5). The Bible reminds us that all have sinned and need forgiveness (Rom 3:23). If we claim otherwise, we make God out to be a liar and are deceived (1 John 1:8). No doubt Simon was deceived and blind to his need for Christ. Let this not be true of us today.

Second, the woman recognized her need for Christ and was freed from her sinful past. As noted, this woman would have been socially maligned because of her moral shortcomings. Any Jewish rabbi would not have spoken with her, especially in such a public setting. This did not keep her from choosing the right thing and coming to Jesus. Only He could offer her forgiveness and a new life. After all, His mission is to "seek and save the lost" (Luke 19:10). Consequently, she left Jesus forgiven and living in peace. She loved much because she had been forgiven much (7:47–48, 50). We are offered the same grace, mercy, and forgiveness through Christ. No person is outside the scope of salvation. Note Galatians 2:20,

> I have been crucified with Christ. It is no longer I who live, but Christ who lives in me. And the life I now live in the flesh I live by faith in the Son of God, who loved me and gave himself for me.

Note how many times you see first-person pronouns (i.e., "I" and "me"). Salvation was personal to Paul, and it is for us too. God loves each of us and desires for us to be saved (2 Pet 3:9). Let us resolve to come to Jesus because only He can forgive our sins. Every person has a past with sin. Only those forgiven by Christ have a future with Him.

Third, let us not miss the facts in this passage that reveal the true nature of Christ. In this passage, we see the supernatural abilities of Christ. He could read Simon's thoughts (vv. 39–40). He knew this woman's past without asking her (v.

47). Most importantly, He could offer her forgiveness, something only God could do (v. 48). Thus, the people questioned, "Who is this, who even forgives sins?" (v. 49) Jesus's deity is fully displayed in this scene. Simon and his guests may have been confused about Jesus's identity before this meal, but there was no doubt afterward. Jesus showed Himself to be the Son of God and Savior of the world who offers forgiveness, hope, and peace.

CONCLUSION

This passage illustrates well one of the primary themes of Luke's gospel. Jesus offers salvation for all people, no matter their circumstances in life. A woman with a sordid past came to Jesus and left forgiven. When referencing this passage, we often refer to her as the "sinful woman," but perhaps she should be better known as the "forgiven woman." We learn from her example the importance of understanding our need for Christ. When we do, we will be motivated to serve and worship Him.

DISCUSSION QUESTIONS

1. Luke is known as "the gospel for the outcast." How does this passage illustrate this theme? What are some other examples in this account that illustrate this theme?

2. What were some of the social "taboos" that Jesus broke in this passage? What social "taboos" keep us from spreading the gospel to others?

3. How did Simon see Jesus? What kept him from seeing Christ for who He was?

4. Why did the woman respond to Jesus the way she did?

5. What does Jesus mean by "he who is forgiven little, loves little"? How can we keep from having this attitude?

ENDNOTES

[1] Craig Keener, *The IVP Bible Background Commentary,* 2nd ed. (Downers Grove: IVP Academic, 2014), 199.

[2] Robert H. Stein, *Luke,* NAC 24 (Nashville: Broadman and Holman, 1992), 235.

[3] Stein, *Luke*, 236.

[4] Keener, *The IVP Bible Background Commentary*, 199.

[5] James R. Edwards, *The Gospel According to Luke,* PNTC (Grand Rapids: Eerdmans, 2015), 227.

THE EMMAUS ROAD

Joshua Pappas

FOCUS PASSAGE

Luke 24:13–35

ONE MAIN THING

Luke 24:13–35 is fascinating! It shares the account of two confused, disappointed, perhaps even hopeless disciples as they walked together on a journey on the very day of Jesus's resurrection, discussing and debating the monumental events that had occurred. The resurrected Jesus caught up to them and joined both the walk and its conversation. Luke, with inspired skill as an expert storyteller, conveys the facts of the event in a way that provides a powerful witness to Christ's resurrection—and so confirms the Faith and inspires curiosity about what our own resurrected bodies will be like and what we will be capable of in the age to come.

INTRODUCTION

Life is a walk. We use the metaphor often, and so does the Bible. Like walking, living this life means moving through time toward our destinies. The sense of pace varies in different times and places, but time is always passing, so there's always movement toward one of two destinations. Whether we intend to or not, and whether we realize it or not, we all need guidance if we're to reach the right one. We walk through life with a spring in our step when all is well and the news is good—but when bad days bring worse news—feet get heavy, and it can feel like we're not getting anywhere at all. However, the best news of all is the good news of the gospel, and its news is so good it can make even the worst legs of the journey through this life bearable.

Luke 24:13–35 is about a conversation between Jesus and two disciples that took place over a seven-mile walk between Jerusalem and a village called Emmaus on the day of His resurrection. The revelation it provided the two disciples prompted an immediate second walk back the entire distance to Jerusalem. The first walk was with heavy feet. The second had a spring in its step. A life-changing revelation of the resurrected Christ made all the difference in the world for those two disciples. While we wait for Christ's Second Coming, the inspired revelation of the Bible continues to make all the difference in the world to us. We're lost without it.

GOING DEEPER

Let's walk through some of the text together. Verse 13 starts with "That very day" (ESV). This means it was the

Lord's Day, Sunday—the very day Jesus rose from the dead. "Two of them" looks back to Verse 9, where we're told the women who found the tomb empty, "told all these things to the eleven *and to all the rest*" (italics mine). So, two of the disciples who had heard the women's report about the empty tomb were walking the seven-mile journey from Jerusalem to Emmaus. Seven miles is about a two-and-a-half hour walk at a brisk pace over level ground. The region around Jerusalem is the central highlands of Israel. The terrain is hilly and rugged, and the two disciples' feet were heavy with discouragement, so there's no telling how long the journey took. Luke tells us one of them was named Cleopas. The other is not named in the text. As they walked, they were discussing the things that had happened, which included the betrayal, arrest, abuse, death, and burial of Jesus as well as the day's confusing reports about the empty tomb and Jesus being alive again from the dead.

It's at this point that verses 15 and 16 say Jesus walked up and joined the conversation but that "their eyes were kept from recognizing Him" (ESV). Some have assumed there was something so apparently different about Jesus's appearance after His resurrection that He couldn't be recognized by those who had known Him before His death without help. There is no clear reason in any of the gospels to conclude Jesus's resurrected body had different proportions or features than those He had before His death. R. T. France writes, "The language in Greek here is quite forceful: 'Their eyes were overpowered.'"[1] Divine power concealed Christ's identity from them just as it formerly shielded their minds from understanding what He had clearly said about His betrayal and death before the fact (cf. Luke 9:45). He had spoken clearly then, and

they couldn't understand. His appearance was recognizable
here, but they couldn't perceive it. In both cases, the
perception problem was ultimately spiritual, not physical.
The truth was hidden from their eyes because of unbelief.
In John 20:16, Mary Magdalene, for whatever reason, only
turned to look at Jesus when He called her by name, and
when she did, she recognized Him immediately. In His
resurrection, Jesus was (and is) still Jesus—recognizably so
—or else the eyewitnesses would have had reason to
doubt. Thank God they had no reason to doubt.

The gospels provide credible eyewitness testimony to
the fact of the resurrection.

> Now Jesus did many other signs in the presence of the
> disciples, which are not written in this book; but these
> are written so that you may believe that Jesus is the
> Christ, the Son of God, and that by believing you may
> have life in his name (John 20:30–31 ESV).

All that was written in the 66 books of the Bible was
confirmed by signs and wonders (Heb 2:1–4). We have
every reason to believe with assurance. "Faith means being
sure of the things we hope for and knowing that something is real even if we do not see it" (Heb 11:1 NCV).

But I think the way the Lord chose to reveal Himself
to Cleopas and company teaches us something about our
relationship with Him that is especially applicable to us
today, now that He has ascended out of our sight into
heaven (cf. 1 Pet 1:3–12). Though we do not now see Christ
with our mortal eyes, God reveals Him as alive and well, as
Savior and King to all who seek Him through trust in the
testimony of the written word and promises us all that He
will come again and rescue us from every evil, including

death (cf. 1 Cor 15:25–26, 51–57). It is through the ministry of the written word that we find all faithful disciples in the world gathered into local church bodies on the first day of every week to break bread together in holy communion. When we do, through the message the Lord's Supper conveys, we "proclaim the Lord's death until he comes" (1 Cor 11:26 ESV). If we proclaim His death, we also proclaim His resurrection because the tomb is empty. Thus, Jesus revealed Himself in the breaking of bread to the eyes of the two disciples, and He reveals Himself to our hearts today when we break bread in church with understanding.

APPLICATION

1. The first and arguably most important lesson we should draw from Luke 24:13–35 is the most straightforward one. Jesus rose from the dead bodily and revealed Himself to multiple eyewitnesses, even in groups, and the gospels now furnish their testimony to every subsequent generation. "So faith comes from hearing, and hearing through the word of Christ" (Rom 10:17 ESV). The tomb was empty. That was a fact. The women had testified to the truth of it, and the Twelve had not believed them. The fact that the gospels all agree Jesus appeared first to women is strong proof of the truthfulness of the resurrection accounts because the First Century world did not regard a woman's testimony as equal to a man's. If the story was fabricated, the first witnesses would have been men. Cleopas and the unnamed disciple did not believe the sisters' report any more than the apostles had. They "had hoped" Jesus was more than just a prophet but had given up that hope. They weren't prepared to see Jesus because of unbelief, and perhaps this is why divine power kept

them from recognizing Him for so long. Notice that after
Jesus had schooled them in Old Testament Messianic
Prophecy for what must have been blissful hours (don't we
all wish we had a transcript of that conversation?), He
made to move on. Job done. The testimony of Scripture
alone is sufficient evidence to create and sustain faith in
Christ. I'll say it again. The testimony of Scripture alone is
sufficient evidence to create and sustain faith in Christ (cf.
Luke 16:31). There is no excuse for unbelief! It was only
when the written word had done its work on their hearts
that they begged Him to stay. As He (remarkably) assumed
the role of host and head of the table in who knows whose
house and broke the bread just as He had done in insti-
tuting the Lord's Supper three days earlier, their unbelief
melted away, the divine power over their eyes was lifted,
and they became believers. They immediately hastened
back the whole distance to Jerusalem, most likely arriving
well after dark, to share the news, and found that the Lord
had appeared to Cephas as well. The account of the seven-
mile walk to Emmaus proves that the Jews who rejected
Jesus as Messiah did so because they did not understand
their own Scriptures. The same remains true today. Luke
makes it clear that the gospel of Jesus Christ is the true
meaning of, total fulfillment of, and proper continuation of
the story of the Law and the Prophets and the Writings,
which, together, compose the whole of the Old Testament.

2. A second application of Luke 24:13–35 has to do with
the nature of Jesus's resurrected body and has generated
no small amount of wonder among believers over the
centuries. We have already seen that His body was His
body, that is, the same one that was buried was the one
that was raised, still recognizable by those who knew Him
but changed in nature. It was and remains a physical body

(cf. Col 2:9). He invited eyewitnesses to touch Him (Luke 24:39). He ate food with them (Luke 24:41–43). But His new deathless body no longer has the limitations of physicality as we understand it as mortals. He could disappear and reappear anywhere. He could pass through locked doors (John 20:19, 26). The apostle John tells us in no uncertain terms that when our bodies are raised from the dead on the Last Day, we will be like Him (1 John 3:2). We will have no problem seeing Him for who and what He is on that day. His resurrection is the first fruit of which ours will follow in kind (1 Cor 15:23). We cannot now fully imagine what it will be like to be in bodies that are superior to death and no longer bound by the laws of physics, but we should try until our hearts are filled with the wonder of hope, and we have determined, along with the apostle Paul, to

> count everything as loss because of the surpassing worth of knowing Christ Jesus ... that [we] may know him and the power of his resurrection, and may share his sufferings, becoming like him in his death, that by any means possible [we] may attain the resurrection from the dead (Phil 3:8–11 ESV).

Nothing else will matter in the end if we are not in Christ, but if the last trumpet finds us faithful, the truth will outshine every imagination. Whatever loyalty to Jesus costs you, pay it. It will be more than worth it in the end.

CONCLUSION

Life is a walk. Living this life means moving through time toward our destinies at an ever-changing pace. The pace varies, but there's always movement toward one of two destinations, and we all need guidance from the Bible if we're to reach the right one. We all prefer it when all is well, the news is good, and we walk with a spring in our step. But the truth that Jesus's tomb is empty and that through faith in Him, ours will be too one day soon, makes even the bad days that bring worse news bearable. Because He arose and reigns and has promised to rescue us even from death, we have every reason to keep moving forward in faith, joyful even in suffering, because the victory is won and eternal life in glory is more certain than the rising and setting of the sun. Praise God!

What a conversation Cleopas and his partner must have had with Jesus! Their hearts burned within them as He opened the Scriptures to them, interpreting everything in them about Himself. We wish we could go back in time and walk along with them. That's not going to happen, of course, but by the grace of the Holy Spirit, we have the completed canon of Scripture. **The Bible still testifies all about Jesus, and by dedicating ourselves to prayerful study, there is not one truth Jesus shared with Cleopas that He will not share with us.** May we all realize this and never forget it. And, whatever our walks through this mortal life might bring, let us resolve ourselves in faith to walk with Jesus all the way. Walking with Him leads to immortality.

DISCUSSION QUESTIONS

1. In the passage, Cleopas and his companion initially walked with heavy hearts and disbelief. What factors contributed to their

discouragement, and how did their encounter with the resurrected Jesus transform them? How can we apply this to our own lives when facing challenges?

2. The text mentions that their eyes were "kept from recognizing" Jesus (Luke 24:16). What do you think this means, and why do you believe Jesus chose not to reveal His identity immediately to them? How might this relate to our experiences of recognizing Jesus in our lives?

3. The passage highlights the importance of the Scriptures in revealing Jesus to Cleopas and his companion. How does the Old Testament point to Jesus as the Messiah and Savior? How can we deepen our understanding of Jesus through the study of the Old Testament?

4. The text emphasizes the nature of Jesus's resurrected body, which was both physical and capable of transcending physical limitations. How does the concept of the resurrection and our future resurrected bodies impact our faith and hope as Christians? How can we live with this hope in mind in our present lives?

ENDNOTE

[1] R.T. France, *Luke*, Teach the Text Commentary Series (Grand Rapids: Baker Books, 2013), 861, Everand ed.

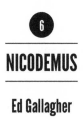

NICODEMUS

Ed Gallagher

FOCUS PASSAGE

John 3:1–15

ONE MAIN THING

Nicodemus serves as an example of a budding disciple who experiences fear and confusion and, nevertheless, presses ahead with Jesus.[1]

INTRODUCTION

Let's start with some controversy. On June 7, 2020, James Bennett resigned from his job at the *New York Times*. He was the editorial page editor who had invited Republican Senator Tom Cotton to write an essay responding to the "mostly peaceful" protests occurring at that time in cities throughout the United States, sparked by video of a Minneapolis police officer kneeling on the neck of a man for nine minutes, leading to the man's death. The *Times* published Cotton's essay on June 3 under the title, "Send In the Troops." Cotton argued that federal troops should be employed to quell the riots and protect people and businesses. There was an immediate uproar among staff at the *Times* who proclaimed that publishing the *op-ed* endangered their lives. The publisher of the *Times*, A. G. Sulzberger, after initially backing his editorial page editor, asked for his resignation less than a week after Cotton's essay appeared.[2]

Almost every sentence of the above paragraph contains multiple opportunities for misunderstanding and disagreement, and the issues stir lively debate. Or, at least, I hope so. Because among all the issues raised by the end of Bennett's tenure at the *Times*, one of the most important is the value of debating ideas, of considering varying points of view, and formulating responses. These days the people that used to be called liberals (at least, a lot of them) have adopted a distinctively illiberal stance toward ideas they don't like. "Not only do I reject your ideas, not only do I refuse to even attempt to refute your ideas, not only do I refuse to listen to your ideas, but I proclaim that the airing of your ideas is dangerous and therefore should not be allowed." Let's not pretend that the situation is any better on the right, among the people who used to be called conservatives (or, at least, a lot of them) but have now adopted their own brand of illiberalism. No need to develop a response to ideas; all I have to do is preemptively declare that those ideas represent an existential threat to the future of life, liberty, and the pursuit of happiness and so should be attacked by those who know what time it is—of course in a "mostly peaceful" way.

This aspect of our modern culture reminds me of the situation in John 7 when the Pharisees sent officers to arrest Jesus because he was saying things they didn't like. The officers returned empty-handed, partly because they actually listened to the words of Jesus (John 7:45–46). The Pharisees were incredulous, proclaiming that their own commitment to the Torah, the Jewish law, was what prevented them from being duped by Jesus like the ignorant crowds (7:49). It was at that moment that Nicodemus courageously pushed back, asking whether the Torah—to which the Pharisees were so committed—permitted the condemnation of people without first hearing them (7:50; cf. Deut 19:16–18). We, readers of John's Gospel, recognize that this is the main problem with the Jewish leadership throughout the Gospel: a refusal to listen, to consider the words of Jesus rather than preemptively categorizing his words as dangerous in order to justify eliminating the threat. In that context, the Gospel presents to us Nicodemus, who is perhaps not the ideal disciple but has a couple of essential qualities of a disciple: the willingness to listen and the courage to prod others to do the same.

GOING DEEPER

Okay, Nicodemus is not the most courageous character in John's Gospel (that would be Jesus). The fact that he first approaches Jesus at night (John 3:2) perhaps reveals some fear on his part. Yet, he does approach Jesus, and he has obviously been paying attention. "Rabbi, we know that you are a teacher who has come from God; for no one can do these signs that you do apart from the presence of God" (3:2). Nicodemus says that "we" know that Jesus must be from God. Who's "we"? He is introduced to us as a Pharisee, a leader of the Jews (3:1). I reckon that some of the other Pharisees have come to the same realization as

Nicodemus. This meeting with Nicodemus takes place in Jerusalem, immediately after Jesus cleansed the temple (2:13–23). The Gospel does not tell us about any signs that Jesus had performed in Jerusalem by this time; so far the Gospel has reported only a single sign, the miracle at the wedding feast in Cana, far from Jerusalem (2:1–12). Later, the Gospel informs us that Jesus did a whole bunch of stuff not recorded here (21:25). Apparently Jesus had been performing signs in Jerusalem, signs observed by Nicodemus and some other Pharisees. Indeed, at the Passover, "many believed in his name because they saw the signs that he was doing" (2:23). Among Nicodemus and his friends, Jesus had become a topic of conversation. Some of the Pharisees had started discussing his work and his identity. "He must be from God. Who is he? Can he be ... you know. Someone needs to talk to him, see what sort of message God has given him." (Remember that earlier John the Baptist had also been questioned by a delegation, John 1:19.) Maybe Nicodemus just drew the short straw, but I think he probably volunteered. He was intrigued enough to desire the personal encounter instead of waiting on a report from a third party.

He wasn't ready to keep up with Jesus. (Who is?) Jesus immediately told Nicodemus what he needed to hear, what he had probably been sent to discover: the path toward the kingdom of God. Jesus told him that entering the kingdom of God would require a new birth. Nicodemus was completely baffled and never recovered, not in this conversation, anyway. His last comment in John 3 is the bewildered (frustrated?) cry, "How can these things be?" (3:9).

Nicodemus was brave enough to approach Jesus, though not so brave to do so during the daytime.

Nicodemus was ready to listen, but he wasn't prepared for what he heard.

Jesus told him that he needed a new birth in order to enter the kingdom of God. Nicodemus realized that Jesus couldn't be talking about a literal birth (John 3:4), but he didn't understand what else Jesus could mean. So Jesus explained further: entering the kingdom of God requires that one be born of water and the Spirit (3:5). This explanation is itself sufficiently mysterious that it has provoked a variety of interpretations. Many people have seen a reference to baptism here, including one of the earliest interpreters of this story, Justin Martyr in the second century, who quoted John 3:5 in a discussion of baptism (*First Apology* 61). The question remains whether Nicodemus would have been able to perceive that Jesus was talking about baptism, and there are other possibilities for what "water" signifies here (maybe amniotic fluid? maybe a reference to the Spirit, such that "water and Spirit" is a hendiadys?).[3] Yet, the Gospel has already shown us people getting baptized (1:25–26), including Jesus (1:29–34), and that is also the context of the story immediately following Jesus's encounter with Nicodemus (3:22). We have already seen that early readers of John's Gospel (or, at least one of them) thought of baptism when they read about being born of water and the Spirit.

But Jesus wanted Nicodemus to understand something more profound than simply the necessity of baptism. The kingdom of God is not susceptible to normal life. As one of Jesus's followers would later put it, "flesh and blood cannot inherit the kingdom of God" (1 Cor 15:50). What Jesus demands from people is nothing short of a new birth, a birth from above, characterized by the divine Spirit's activity within the person. Readers of John's Gospel are not as surprised as was Nicodemus because we have the advantage of having read the Gospel's opening statement, containing these words:

> Whoever received him, he gave to them the ability to become children of God, to those believing in his name, who were born not from blood or from the will of flesh or from the will of a man but from God (John 1:12–13).

What Jesus demands is not just a ritual to "get in," but a different kind of life—a life like that of Jesus himself, on whom the divine Spirit remained from the time of his baptism, as John the Baptist testified (John 1:32; cf. 3:34). The Spirit gives life (6:63), as the apostle Paul also declared (Rom 8:1–11), and therefore also the Spirit determines whether someone has the new birth that identifies one as a child of God (John 1:34; Rom 8:14–17).

APPLICATION

On the one hand, there is the message of Jesus, and, on the other hand, there's the response from Nicodemus. Both have lessons for us. John 3 contains the most famous verse in this Gospel (not to mention the entire Bible), a verse that declares God's love for the world resulting in everlasting life for those who believe in God's Son (John 3:16). Jesus came to impart life, and no Gospel makes that aim more clear than the Fourth Gospel. The Greek word for "life" (ζωή, *zoē*) appears thirty-six times in John and only sixteen times total in the Synoptic Gospels. Whereas the other Gospels talk about "the kingdom of God/heaven," John's Gospel uses this phrase only twice—only in Jesus's speech to

Nicodemus—and instead emphasizes life. In other words, when Jesus talks about "life" in the Fourth Gospel, He means (almost?) the same thing as what He means by "kingdom" in the other Gospels. (The connection between life and kingdom is made also in, e.g., Mark 10:17, 23.) The concept of a new life in Jesus, and thus a new birth to experience this new life, is shown to be mysterious in John 3. That seems to be the point of verse 8. But without the new birth, one cannot even see the kingdom of God (verse 3). One must follow the Spirit's lead, especially now through the Scriptures that he inspired. Not emphasized in Jesus's remarks to Nicodemus, but emphasized in Scripture, is the fact that the new life requires new living, that there are strict ethical demands for one guided by the Spirit and not by the flesh. (See again Romans 8; also Galatians 5:13–26.)

What about Nicodemus's response? I've already mentioned that he was baffled, bewildered, maybe frustrated. But, most importantly, he listened. He engaged. He knew he needed to hear what Jesus wanted to tell him, even if it was a struggle. He did not respond to the difficult words of Jesus like the disciples of John 6: "This is a hard saying; who can listen to it? ... After this many of his disciples turned back and no longer walked with him" (6:60, 66). To be sure, I don't know whether Nicodemus ever walked with Jesus, but it seems to me that he was always moving toward Jesus, never away from Him. We have already seen that after his first, difficult encounter with Jesus, he spoke up against hasty and baseless condemnations of Jesus promoted by his fellow Pharisees and received blowback from them (7:50–52). Nicodemus seems to me someone not fully committed but who was interested, someone willing to listen despite the objections of his colleagues, and that attitude is a necessary precondition to the new birth about which Jesus spoke.[4]

CONCLUSION

Nicodemus appears three times in the Bible: John 3:1–9; 7:50–52; 19:38–42. We have considered the first two passages. The final passage shows Nicodemus with Joseph of Arimathea arranging for the burial of Jesus. The Gospel writer identifies Joseph as a disciple of Jesus who kept his faith hidden out of fear; while no such evaluation is offered for Nicodemus, the same thing could probably be said about him. Being a secret disciple is not ideal, and, as I mentioned earlier, no one would accuse Nicodemus (or Joseph) of being an ideal disciple. But each of the three appearances of Nicodemus in this Gospel seems (to me, at least) to show him growing in his commitment to Jesus—from willing to listen, to cautious defense, to a more public show of respect (the burial). The Gospel leaves us wondering whatever happened to Nicodemus: Did he continue to grow in faith, or did fear best him? I am unaware of early Christian tradition about Nicodemus outside the Bible, though he is venerated as a saint in Catholic and Orthodox churches.

Pondering the faith of Nicodemus ought to lead us to ponder our faith, which is entirely the Gospel's point in narrating this encounter with Jesus. Nicodemus listened. Will we? Jesus wants to tell us some things. The examples all around us teach us to refuse to listen to things that we find offensive, to things we just don't want to hear. The message Jesus brought is necessarily offensive. "I am the way, the truth, and the life" (John 14:6). Refusing to consider policy proposals in a modern American context might have some serious consequences for our lives or perhaps the nation—but that's relatively small potatoes in comparison to the issues that concern us here. Jesus is The Way. The Truth. The Life. There are things He wants to tell us that we find hard to hear. One of those things is probably that a nice, comfortable, normal life will prevent us from seeing the kingdom of God. Nicodemus listened —and kept moving toward Jesus. Will we?

DISCUSSION QUESTIONS

1. Does Nicodemus come to Jesus in John 3 as a believer or an unbeliever?
2. If you were in the shoes of Nicodemus, do you think you would have such a hard time understanding Jesus?
3. What does Jesus want people to know about the new birth?
4. What do you make of Nicodemus's words in John 7:50–51? Is he defending Jesus? What are his motivations?
5. Does Nicodemus provide a good example for Christians today?

ENDNOTES

[1] I appreciate Elaine Brown's help with this essay.

[2] See Bennett's account of this episode in his essay, "When the New York Times Lost Its Way," *The Economist* (Dec 14, 2023).

[3] For various possibilities, see Richard Bauckham,

Gospel of Glory: Major Themes in Johannine Theology (Grand Rapids: Baker, 2015), 82–90.

[4] My reading of Nicodemus is more positive than those often presented in scholarship on the Gospel of John. For different depictions, see R. Alan Culpepper, "Nicodemus: The Travail of New Birth," in *Character Studies in the Fourth Gospel: Narrative Approaches to Seventy Figures in John*, ed. Steven A. Hunt, D. Francois Tolmie, and Ruben Zimmermann (Tübingen: Mohr Siebeck, 2013), 249–59; Cornelis Bennema, *Encountering Jesus: Character Studies in the Gospel of John*, 2d ed. (Minneapolis: Fortress, 2014), 147–60. On whether there might be extra-biblical information about Nicodemus, see Richard Bauckham, *The Testimony of the Beloved Disciple: Narrative, History, and Theology in the Gospel of John* (Grand Rapids: Baker, 2007), 137–72.

7

THE WOMAN AT THE WELL

Thomas Tidwell

FOCUS PASSAGE

John 4:1–21

Imagine that you were teleported back to first-century Palestine. You are outside the city of Sychar, in Samaria, and you are a follower of Jesus. His disciples have gone into the city to get food, and you are near the well of water that Jacob dug many centuries before. You see a woman getting water for her needs, and Jesus asks for a drink of water.

As you watch, He cares enough to talk one-on-one with a woman from Samaria.

The woman draws some water from the well, and Jesus asks for a drink of water. It is not a big deal, but there is some banter over the fact that Jesus is a Jew, and she—a Samaritan. Jewish men would never ask for water from a woman from Samaria. It would make them "unclean." Yet, with a common need for water, Jesus used this as an opportunity to talk with the woman about her greatest need—the need for the gospel.

Coming back to our day and age, we see that there are many people today who are looking for hope—looking for something beyond the toils and trials of this life. Many go to work daily to a monotonous job, and despair of ever getting something better. They have resigned themselves to mediocrity, to jobs that have no hope of improving, to families that have their struggles daily just to make ends meet. Notice how Jesus confronted this woman, a woman who may have been without any hope of things getting better in her life.

JESUS NEEDED TO GO THROUGH SAMARIA.

He needed to go through Samaria (John 4:4). Was it because it was a shorter distance to go through Samaria than to walk around Samaria? Perhaps. The Jews hated the Samaritans, and the Samaritans reciprocated, so it would have been odd that a Jewish rabbi would go through Samaria instead of around it.

We must remember that Jesus did not come to save only the Jews, but all mankind. The racial, socioeconomic, and gender divides in our country are nothing new; they have been in existence since man was created by God and placed on earth. As Christians, we must make sure we don't look at a person's skin color or ethnicity, we must not consider their possessions; we must see people as God sees them—souls lost and without hope unless they come to Jesus.

Consider as well the various views about women at that time. The Jews and others thought of women as keepers at home and thus, second-class citizens. Add to these facts the idea that this woman had had five husbands, and *"the one you now have is not your husband"* (John 4:16–18). She probably avoided others because of the situation in which she found herself due to bad decisions on her part, or things out of her control. Thus, she was getting water in the heat of the day, so as to avoid the looks, smirks, whispers, and judgments of her life's choices. Can we begin to understand the prejudice against women in that day, especially when we see the "kind of woman" she was?

Jesus needed to go through Samaria, to teach and help this woman, as well as the souls of the Samaritans. They had great misunderstandings of Messiah, believing that He would come to the mountain on which they worshipped and vindicate them as opposed to the Jews. Messiah did come to give them eternal life, as He did with the Jews. But their prejudices, ideas, and animosity kept them from seeing a Jewish Messiah.

Further, Jesus needed to rest. We appreciate these tidbits in Scripture to remind us that He was just like us as humans. He grew tired, weary, angry . . . yet did not sin. He took time to rest. He took time to commune with God, but always remembered His mission—to seek and save the lost (Luke 19:10). Even when He rested, He thought about the souls of others. Do we?

THE SAMARITAN WOMAN'S RESPONSE

When Jesus asked the Samaritan woman for water, she could not resist pointing out the fact that He was a Jew and she was a Samaritan. Yet, both had the same needs as humans. They needed water to drink. Jesus took that need and turned it into a teaching opportunity. As we have the heart of Jesus in trying to teach others the gospel, we need to start with common ground — we are all humans, we all have souls, and we all have needs that only the living water (Jesus) can provide. Her soul was as precious to Jesus as that of any Jewish man or woman. Do I see people with souls for whom Christ died? Do I see their need for the gospel? We must see the lost as being outside of God's grace and love, and consider where they will spend eternity before we will ever share the gospel with them.

This is where we begin when we talk to others about Jesus; when we help others encounter the gospel. We find common ground and use that as a way to meet the greatest need of people—the need for salvation from sin.

We understand that when we try to teach someone the gospel, many will react just like this woman. She did not want to talk about her sinful situation with the man "*she was now with*" (John 4:16–18), so she tried to change the subject. Her new topic was worship. Where should we worship—on this mountain or with the Jews in Jerusalem? Many we teach today want to know about worship (such as instrumental music), but we must not begin with that. We must share the gospel story of Jesus—and discuss these other things later.

Jesus teaches us vital lessons on how to handle a discussion when we are faced with a "change in the subject." Jesus told her that she did not know God, and He emphasized that salvation was of the Jews. He did not tone it down, nor did He change the truth, because He wanted to gain her acceptance. He did teach true worshippers will worship in spirit and in truth because "*God is spirit and those who worship him must worship in spirit and truth*." (John 4:24).

Jesus then plainly tells her that He is the Messiah.

Hence, He has the right to dictate the terms of worship as well as salvation.

What are some things we see in Jesus's discussion with the woman at the well?

First, we need to talk about things we have in common, then kindly lead to a discussion of the gospel.

Second, we need to talk about needs, not wants. Man's greatest need is salvation from sin and a relationship with God that will last eternally.

Third, we need to talk about this relationship with God daily. The greatest relationship that we should work on is our relationship with God. Our relationship with God determines our relationships with others. When we place our relationship with God FIRST, it will help us to be better husbands, wives, children, parents, workers, and Christians. We remember that God has given His church to help us have better Christian relationships here on earth, to encourage and help one another be better and stronger Christians, but also to help those who are not Christians to become Christians so they, too, can find hope in a hopeless world.

Fourth, we need to start with people where they are, not where we want them to be. Jesus started with this woman where she was and led her to not only follow Him but also to share with others that she had met Jesus, the Messiah.

THE DISCIPLES' RESPONSE

The disciples want to know why Jesus was talking with a SAMARITAN WOMAN. Much like the disciples then, we often allow our prejudices to get in the way of sharing the gospel. This was apparent as the disciples *". . . marveled that he was talking with a woman . . .*" Sometimes we make snap judgments that "excuse us" from having these hard conversations with others about their souls. This teaches us that all need to hear the gospel, and we need to help them to know Christ.

THE WOMAN SPREADS THE NEWS (JOHN 4:28–29).

When we are saved, we want to tell others. The message was about "*A man who told me all I ever did*" (John 4:39). Always point to Jesus! It is never about us; it is about what Jesus does. Earlier she was ashamed and avoided people, but talking with the Master made her courageous. When we become Christians, we want everyone to know, but as time goes on, the zeal wanes, life comes crashing back in, and we get distracted and discouraged. We forget that we have a role to play in sharing the gospel with others! Jesus's work is our work.

WHAT WAS JESUS'S WORK?

"*I must do the will of him that sent me, to finish his work*" (John 4:34). Do we strive to finish the work? How often do we get sidetracked? How often do we come close to finishing —but quit? Many Christians start strong and then fall away (some more quickly than others); we need to start strong and stay strong for the souls of loved ones and friends, and for our own salvation.

WE MUST FINISH HIS WORK.

Now is the time to harvest souls—we always have time for things of this world—but we do not take time for evangelism. Souls are at stake. Sow the seed; we never know when it will produce a yield. Allow God's word to convert people to Christ. Sow the seed. Someone else may reap, but sow the seed. The Samaritans believed because of the word of the woman. They then listened to Jesus and many more believed because of His word.

WE KNOW THAT THIS IS INDEED THE CHRIST, THE SAVIOR OF THE WORLD.

DISCUSSION QUESTIONS

1. What did you learn from this lesson about Jesus?
2. Do I walk, think, and see what Jesus does?
3. What is my response to someone who is not a Christian? How can I change my attitude to be used by Jesus even more?
4. What lessons did you learn from this text in John when it comes to evangelism?
5. What will you do to help fulfill Jesus's great commission?
6. What can you do to be like Jesus in finishing his work?
7. Will you be faithful until you finish your work?

THE ADULTERESS

Tim Martin

FOCUS PASSAGE

John 7:53–8:11

ONE MAIN THING

Unmerited mercy

INTRODUCTION

The pericope of John 7:53–8:11 is replete with external and internal issues. Despite these obstacles, the passage provides lessons about mercy, forgiveness, and exhortation which are valuable to Jesus-followers of the twenty-first-century church. Working through the textual and theological challenges is a worthwhile exegetical and critical exercise, but one must also focus on the summation of the story. In the end, Jesus demonstrated God's mercy in the earthly realm to a woman who had indeed sinned, but also a human being who had been used as a pawn by the Jewish religious aristocracy to serve their own burning jealousy towards Jesus.

GOING DEEPER

From the external perspective, nearly every modern translation offsets this passage within brackets or contains a footnote regarding the lack of manuscript (MS) evidence supporting its originality to the Fourth Gospel. Space does not allow for a full treatment of this controversy in this work. However, it is pertinent to summarize the evidence and opinions regarding the MS traditions in which this passage is absent and those where it is included. English translators often note John 7:53–8:11 is not present in the "earliest manuscripts" and the "most ancient authorities," or they comment that "later manuscripts add" the account. These statements are accurate since this pericope is absent in the oldest witnesses to John's Gospel, the third-century papyri P66 and P75. It is also missing in some of the oldest NT majuscules, the fourth-century codices Siniaticus (ℵ) and Vaticanus (B) and the fifth-century uncials Alexandrinus (A), Ephraemi Rescriptus (C), and Washingtonius (W).[1] The earliest attestation for John 7:53–8:11 is the fifth-century Greek–Latin diglot, Codex Bezae (D). The bulk of the MS evidence supporting the inclusion of this encounter in John comes primarily from manuscripts (MSS) from the Middle Ages, Latin versions, and the Western textual and patristic tradition.[2] Some MSS include it at other locations in John while others place it in the Gospel of Luke.[3]

Although the external evidence does not support this

testing of Jesus as being original to the autographic text of John, "most Western church traditions consider it canonical, authoritative for Christian theology, and worthy to be read as Scripture."[4] Many scholars who have concluded the passage is a later addition to the Fourth Gospel also recognize its strong presence in the oral tradition, Western patristic writings, and ancient versions.[5] Craig L. Blomberg rightly observes that, despite their text-critical skepticism, "many scholars nevertheless suggest that it may reflect a genuine episode from Jesus' life, preserved in the oral tradition, and later added to the text by Christian scribes."[6] Bruce M. Metzger agreed, commenting that "the account has all the earmarks of historical accuracy" and "it is obviously a piece of oral tradition which circulated in certain parts of the Western church and which was subsequently incorporated into various manuscripts at various places."[7]

It also fits well with Jesus's other encounters with the Jewish religious leadership who consistently attempted to trap Jesus with challenging questions.[8] The scribes and Pharisees, as was their habit, attacked Jesus's honor and his loyalty to God, but "Jesus chooses to defend his honor by dishonoring his challengers."[9] George R. Beasley-Murray, commenting on Jesus's response to His challengers, states "there is no reason to doubt" the "substantial truth" of this pericope and "the saying that it preserves is completely in character with what we know of our Lord."[10] As was the case for all of the schemes used to force Jesus into a doctrinal or political dilemma, this attempt failed miserably. In fact, in His response, "the word of Jesus challenged their life in the sight of God, and they failed the test."[11]

The internal challenges to understanding this encounter also evade easy explanation. Although many solutions have been proposed, no one has any idea what Jesus wrote when he stooped down and scrawled in the dirt. Perhaps John D. Meade and Peter J. Gurry present a fitting proposal, noting Jesus wrote with His finger on the ground "just as God wrote the Ten Words" and "the point is that Jesus, unlike this woman's accusers, has the same divine authority as God, and this makes his mercy all the more remarkable."[12] If this story was a manufactured folktale, one must ask why the editor would not have described what Jesus wrote. If this pericope is "not attributable to an eyewitness" then this and the other oddities in this passage "point to a storyteller eminently skilled at creating a dramatic effect."[13] It is much more likely the challenging and mysterious nature of John 7:53–8:11 is due to it being a record of an actual historical event during Jesus's ministry. There are many accounts in the Bible that prove the adage "truth is stranger than fiction."

One of the most glaring issues is the absence of the co-defendant, the male counterpart in this affair. According to the Torah, both participants in an adulterous affair are subject to capital punishment.[14] If she was indeed "caught in adultery," then it is absurd to think the identity of the male participant was unknown to these accusers. Scholars differ on the role of the woman in this situation. Was she someone's wife or betrothed to a man and was having sex with another married or single man? Perhaps she was a single woman who had been caught having sex with a married man. Either way, it is odd the other party was not also dragged before Jesus.[15] A third possibility, albeit unlikely, is the supposed "adulteress" was in fact complicit as part of a farce concocted by the scribes and Pharisees, there had not actually been any act of adultery, and her participation in the sham was her act of "sin" Jesus forgave.[16] This theory would explain another theological conundrum: why Jesus did not rule in favor of punishing the woman with death as the Torah plainly prescribes. However, Jesus had been known to show flexibility in matters of Torah, especially for the charge of Sabbath-breaking by His own disciples. This offense clearly merited death by stoning as seen in Numbers 15:32–36. Whether Jesus's disciples violated the Sabbath and what constituted a violation is a debate for another time.

These vicious scribes and Pharisees are consumed with destroying Jesus's credibility. This woman was "being instrumentalized" as a pawn by Jesus's opponents as "in a situation of considerable distress, half-clad, and aware that she is facing death, the woman is of no concern to the scribes and Pharisees" and she has simply "become chattel in a legal debate."[17] These unscrupulous men are shaming the woman in order to accomplish their goals, and "her personal life is incidental."[18] Micheals finds the woman takes "center stage as the accused" and "a kind of surrogate for Jesus himself."[19]

When asked about whether the prescribed sentence should be carried out, Jesus's curt response did not imply a requirement of perfection on behalf of the accusers, but was in fact, based on the Torah:

> On the evidence of two witnesses or of three witnesses the one who is to die shall be put to death; a person shall not be put to death on the evidence of one witness. The hand of the witnesses shall be first against him to put

him to death, and afterward the hand of all the people.
So you shall purge the evil from your midst. (Deut 17:6–
7, ESV)

He never implied any innocence on behalf of the
accused but forced her accusers and the witnesses to
consider their own high-handedness. They were also guilty
parties, conspiring to entrap Jesus in a snare that they
vainly hoped would discredit the Galilean troublemaker
and serve their own selfish purposes. Slowly, one at a time,
the conspirators exited the scene. It was not Jesus who was
pushed into a proverbial theological corner, but His opponents who no longer had the mettle to carry out the
barbaric execution of this woman.

Jesus's final dismissive remarks to the accused woman
are the true crux of this narrative. As a matter of fact,
"instead of Jesus being judged and vindicated, the woman
is judged and vindicated, and her accusers are judged, just
as Jesus' accusers are judged and found wanting in the
Temple discourse as a whole."[20] According to Torah, a case
cannot be adjudicated without a minimum of two or three
witnesses and, once Jesus's response cleared the area, there
were absolutely no witnesses to her alleged crime. In the
end, there were but two, the woman and the one who will
sit on the final throne of judgment, who remained in this
scene.[21] The great judge of the universe acquitted the
woman, something only one with the authority of God
could have done.[22] Jesus showed the woman mercy and
compassion, but also required obedience and righteous
behavior from her in the future. His exhortation for her to
cease her sinful behavior demonstrated that although God
does forgive confessed sins, He does not expect His

people to continue missing the mark of godliness in their conduct.

APPLICATION

Christians often have very high expectations of others while maintaining a lenient and ambivalent attitude toward their own failures. All the supposed witnesses and accusers of the adulterous woman, when asked to assess their own status before God, quickly sobered up to the reality of their own unrighteousness. Burge correctly states "the story of the woman probes our reflexes toward people who do not fit our religious expectations."[23] There is a tendency to view different sins with varying degrees of severity, and to be frank, there are certainly different degrees of punishment for various sins in the Torah. Adultery tends to stir a greater degree of disgust and repulsion due to how much mental, spiritual, and economic damage it incurs. It also represents a sense of betrayal at the most intimate level. However, it can be forgiven by God and by people, although the latter may be more difficult to convince.

CONCLUSIONS

Jesus was forgiving and merciful, therefore Jesus-followers must mimic His behavior and attitude. Modern-day disciples of Christ must reflect on their own shortcomings, including the sins of gossip, slander, greed, drunkenness, and jealousy which occupy the same New Testament "sin lists" as sexual immorality. When one considers the debts of which they have been forgiven and the level of mercy they have been shown, it is much easier to show mercy and forgiveness to others. Scripture demonstrates God has a higher desire for mercy than sacrifice and worship.[24] No one can merit their own forgiveness or earn the mercy of God, any more than the woman in this passage. These things are only available through the graceful gift of Christ's blood on the cross.

DISCUSSION QUESTIONS

1. Does this story, as many scholars assume, have the traits and characteristics of an actual historical encounter with Jesus? Discuss your thoughts about the manuscript evidence and whether it should be considered original to John.
2. Should Jesus have upheld the legal requirements of the Torah and ordered the woman to be stoned to death? Why do you think he decided not to do so?
3. Discuss how this narrative demonstrates Jesus's equality with God, considering not only Jesus's divine authority but also how he reflected different aspects of the nature of God.

ENDNOTES

[1] It should be noted codices A and C are defective in this part of John.

[2] Fuller treatment of the MS evidence can be found in the critical apparatuses for John 7:53–8:11 of the current editions of the Nestle-Aland *Novum Testamentum Graece* (NA28, 322) and United Bible Societies' *The Greek New*

Testament (UBS5, 338). See also Bruce Metzger's analysis in *A Textual Commentary on the Greek New Testament,* 2nd ed. (Stuttgart: Deutsche Bibelgesellschaft, 2002), 187–9. Metzger comments "the evidence for the non-Johannine origin of the pericope of the adulteress is overwhelming" (*A Textual Commentary,* 187).

[3] The twelfth-century minuscules MS 225 and MS 1 place it after John 7:36 and 21:25, respectively. It follows Luke 21:38 in the Family 13 grouping of Greek MSS and after Luke 24:53 in MS 1333 from the eleventh century.

[4] Bruce J. Malina and Richard L. Rohrbaugh, *Social-Science Commentary on the Gospel of John* (Minneapolis: Fortress Press, 1998), 292.

[5] Eusebius refers to a mention of this pericope in the writings of Papias, whose writings date to the late first to early second century, and according to Eusebius, Papias stated the story is contained in the Gospel of the Hebrews (*Hist. eccl.* 3.39.16). Ancient versions, in this context, denote early translations of the NT in Latin, Syriac, Coptic, and other ancient languages.

[6] Craig L. Blomberg, *The Historical Reliability of John's Gospel: Issues and Commentary* (Downers Grove: IVP Academic, 2001), 140.

[7] Metzger, *A Textual Commentary,* 188. Gary M. Burge comments John 7:53–8:11 is "a typical Synoptic 'conflict' story in which Jesus is placed on the horns of a dilemma." *John,* NIVAC (Grand Rapids: Zondervan, 2000), 240.

[8] Blomberg observes the pericope "comports well with the core of historical Jesus material, which so consistently paints him as compassionate towards the outcast, while rebuking the religious establishment of his day" (*The Historical Reliability of John's Gospel,* 140). However, it is worth noting the grouping "scribes and Pharisees" is

absent elsewhere in the Fourth Gospel despite its regularity in the Synoptic Gospels.

[9] Malina and Rohrbaugh, *Social-Science Commentary,* 293.

[10] George R. Beasley-Murray, *John,* 2nd ed., WBC 36 (Mexico City: Thomas Nelson, 2000), 143.

[11] Beasley-Murray, *John,* 146.

[12] John D. Meade and Peter J. Gurry, *Scribes and Scripture: The Amazing Story of How We Got the Bible* (Wheaton: Crossway, 2022), 31.

[13] J. Ramsey Michaels, *The Gospel of John,* NICNT (Grand Rapids: Eerdmans, 2010), 498.

[14] Leviticus 20:10; Deuteronomy 22:22–27.

[15] It has also been suggested the absence of the male is due to misogynistic reasons, i.e., the scribes and Pharisees did not bring in the man because they showed him preferential treatment. This is pure speculation and perhaps even an exegetical overreach that assumes an unfairly low status of women in first-century Palestine.

[16] If Jews did not have the legal authority under Roman hegemony to execute someone for violating their own religious laws (John 18:31–32; contra Acts 7:58–60), then this yields credence to the proposal the entire situation was a ruse. Should Jesus have ordered the adulteress's execution in accordance with Torah, could these Jews have even carried out the sentence? Perhaps, however, the trap itself was to see if Jesus would defy Roman regulations and order her to be stoned or deny the validity of the Torah and dismiss the charges.

[17] Francis J. Moloney, *The Gospel of John,* SP 4 (Collegeville: Liturgical Press, 1998), 260–1.

[18] Burge, *John,* 242.

[19] Michaels, *The Gospel of John,* 495.

[20] Michaels, *The Gospel of John,* 500.

[21] Matthew 25:31–46; John 5:27; 16:8–11; 2 Corinthians 5:10. To be sure, the New Testament authors alternate, and perhaps equivocate, God and Jesus as occupying the eschatological judgment seat (cf. Rom 2:1–5; 14:10; 2 Thess 1:5–12; Rev 20:11–15).

[22] This is certainly not the only instance of Jesus forgiving a person's sins (cf. Matt 9:1–8; Mark 2:1–12; Luke 5:17–26; 7:36–50).

[23] Burge, *John,* 249.

[24] Hosea 6:6; Matthew 9:13; 12:7; 23:23.

BIBLIOGRAPHY

Aland, Kurt, Barbara Aland, Johannes Karavidopoulos, Carlo M. Martini, and Bruce M. Metzger, eds. *Novum Testamentum Graece.* 28th ed. Stuttgart: Deutsche Bibelgesellschaft, 2012.

———. *The Greek New Testament.* 5th ed. Stuttgart: Deutsche Bibelgesellschaft, 2014.

Beasley-Murray, George R. *John.* 2nd ed. WBC 36. Mexico City: Thomas Nelson, 2000.

Blomberg, Craig L. *The Historical Reliability of John's Gospel: Issues and Commentary.* Downers Grove: IVP Academic, 2001.

Burge, Gary M. *John.* NIVAC. Grand Rapids: Zondervan, 2000.

Malina, Bruce J. and Richard L. Rohrbaugh. *Social-Science Commentary on the Gospel of John.* Minneapolis: Fortress Press, 1998.

Meade, John D. and Peter J. Gurry. *Scribes and Scripture: The Amazing Story of How We Got the Bible.* Wheaton: Crossway, 2022.

Metzger, Bruce M. *A Textual Commentary on the Greek*

New Testament. 2nd ed. Stuttgart: Deutsche Bibelge-sellschaft, 2002.

Michaels, J. Ramsey. *The Gospel of John.* NICNT. Grand Rapids: Eerdmans, 2010.

Moloney, Francis J. *The Gospel of John.* SP 4. Collegeville: Liturgical Press, 1998.

THE MAN BORN BLIND

"WHO IS SPIRITUALLY BLIND, AND WHO ISN'T?"

Thomas Tidwell

FOCUS PASSAGE

John 9

In John 9 we see the story of the man born blind as related by the apostle John.

This event has created much discussion about sin, suffering, and why God allows suffering. It helps us to understand issues regarding the "WHY ME?" or "WHY SOMEONE I LOVE?" events. (We need to be reminded that these events will come into all of our lives at one time or another.) It deals with the "why" of suffering—do we inherit our parents' sins? Do we suffer because of the actions of our parents in the past, or do these things happen because we live in a sin-cursed, broken world? The story opens with the disciples asking the Lord, "Rabbi, who sinned, this man or his parents, that he was born blind?" (John 9:2—All quotes in this article will come from the ESV.)

How could a babe in the womb sin and thus be born blind? If sin is a transgression of the law (1 John 3:4–6), how could a babe sin, when he/she has no concept of law, breaking the law, or sinning against God's will? How can they have no clue that there is a God, nor what God's will is, as a babe or a child? Babes need to be taught; hence, God has given parents.

> Jesus answered, "It was not that this man sinned, or his parents, but that the works of God might be displayed in him. We must work the works of him who sent me while it is day; night is coming, when no one can work. As long as I am in the world, I am the light of the world." Having said these things, he spit on the ground and made mud with the saliva. Then he anointed the man's eyes with the mud and said to him, "Go, wash in the pool of Siloam" (which means Sent). So, he went and washed and came back seeing" (John 9:3–5).

Jesus is clear that the reason why this man was born blind was so that ". . . the works of God may be displayed in him."

Jesus healed a man who was born blind and was challenged for doing so on the Sabbath day. The Pharisees, as always, challenged Jesus in every way they could. If they could attack Him and His ideas, they did; if He did not have an answer acceptable to them, they then might be able to shut Jesus up, (at the least), or discredit Him and His teaching. This is what they wanted. Some of them struggled with Jesus healing the man on the Sabbath day, and they couldn't care less THAT the man was healed as much as that it was done on the Sabbath.

The Pharisees and others are still among us today, looking for error to be taught, and hoping for a way to discredit the teacher.

At the same time, they had trouble believing what had happened. How could a man perform a miracle on the Sabbath (which would be work) and still claim that he is from God? Jesus still upsets the world today. His teachings still challenge Christians—and the world!

This text also brings in the question of suffering—do we inherit the repercussions of our parents' sin (or the sins of a previous generation)? Or do we inherit the sin itself? This man was blind from birth. Some religious groups emphasize that sin can be passed down from generation to generation; hence, sin can never really be dealt with. To this writer, it suggests that if sins are inherited, there is no end to sin. Yet Scripture teaches us otherwise about the work of Jesus on the cross. He dealt with the sin problem, once and for all, eternally. We thank God for that!

The blind man was physically dealing with his blindness. Four different groups of people struggled with this issue. Born blind, having no sight was all he knew. He made it clear throughout the exchanges presented—"I was blind, but now I see." He dealt with facts, not wishes or dreams. Facts! (John 9:8–12) The neighbors and the people who knew the man knew he was blind.

The disciples were blinded by prejudice. They *knew* that there was sin involved in the situation in some way. Either his parents had sinned, and the son was having to deal with it, OR the man himself sinned in the womb (see argument above).

Many of the friends and people who heard of the miracle were blinded by skepticism. They were not sure that the man was blind, to begin with, and when they heard the parents say that he had been born blind, there were some doubts as to how long he had had this malady. Some would have dismissed it. Others would have wanted to know all the details before they made their decision. (We will see this with the Pharisees when they asked his parents if he really was blind.)

The Pharisees were blinded by prejudice and hatred. They cared not about the blind man—and many others that Jesus healed while on earth! They hated Jesus for all the times He had rebuked them. They were constantly looking for a way to destroy Him, or at least prove Him wrong, so that the people would continue to follow them and respect their opinions above all. As we read through Scripture, we find them attacking Jesus time and again, being rebuked, and losing the battles time and again. Each time they lost, each time Jesus rebuked them, their hatred would grow, till they "tried Jesus" and brought Him before Pilate! Hatred destroys not only the people hated, but also the haters as well. Contrast this with Jesus and what He came to do!

The blind man's parents were blinded by fear. The Pharisees did not believe the man, nor did they believe the parents when they questioned them, as recorded in John 9:18–23. The Jews did not believe he was blind from birth, so they called on the parents. "Is this your son, who you say was born blind? How does he now see (John 9:18–19)? The parents stated, "We know that this is our son, and that he was born blind. But how he now sees we do not know who opened his eyes. Ask him, he is of age." The parents were afraid of being put out of the synagogue.

We love the blind man and how he stood for Jesus. The Jews then stated to the FORMERLY blind man, "Give glory to God, we know that this man is a sinner" (John 9:24). And the FORMERLY blind man argued, "Whether he is a sinner or not, I do not know.

One thing I know, that though I was blind, now I see." You can't argue the facts!

As the conversation continued, they reviled him, they called him a liar, and they told the formerly blind man that they did not know where Jesus came from. In his unassuming way, he cuts to the heart of the matter:

> It is amazing you do not know him or where he came from AND YET HE OPENED MY EYES. We know God does not listen to sinners, but a worshiper of God is one who does his will, and God listens to him . . . IF THIS MAN WERE NOT FROM GOD, HE COULD DO NOTHING (John 9:33).

We began this study by asking what is more detrimental to man—the man who is physically blind, or the man who is spiritually blind?

Jesus went after the man after he had been cast out of the synagogue. Jesus wants all men to be saved and come to the knowledge of the truth (1 Tim 2:4). After being cast out, while he could now see, his life would be changed because he would not be allowed in the synagogue nor be able to worship publicly with the other Jews. Jesus reassured him that it was okay. Jesus specifically asked,

> Do you believe in the Son of man?
>
> Who is he, sir, that I may believe in Him?
>
> You have seen him, and it is he who is speaking to you.

He said, "Lord, I believe" and he worshipped Him.

Jesus said, "For judgment I came into this world, that those who do not see may see, and those who see may become blind" (John 9:35–39).

Jesus ended the discussion with the Pharisees when they asked, "Are we also blind?"

He answers, "If you were blind you would have no guilt, but now you say we see therefore your guilt remains" (John 9:40–41).

As we reread this passage and how Jesus interacted with the blind man, his parents, the Pharisees, and others, we see Jesus teaching His people today some lessons we need to consider:

1. Do we ourselves personally believe in Jesus enough to obey His commands and honor Him with obedience?

2. Are we blind to what God and Jesus have done to save us?

3. Why is it that those who see "may become blind?"

4. Have we read Scripture enough to recognize Jesus's voice, and to think and act like Jesus?

5. Can you see the possibility of a smile on Jesus's face when He asked the formerly blind man, "You have seen him and it is he who is talking with you"?

6. How many today, especially in the church, are blind because they cannot or will not study God's word enough to know the truth? Do we often listen to teachers who tell us what we like to hear, rather than the truth?

7. The discussion as to who is a sinner is important

even today. Can a sinner do miracles? Jesus performed the miracles; therefore, they should have concluded that Jesus was NOT A SINNER.

a. How do we define sin?

b. How do we understand a miracle? Contrast the religious world today with the miracles in the Bible.

c. How do we judge people whom we don't know by their actions? Are we open enough to listen to their views, and think about their points? Do we summarily dismiss people because they don't agree with us? The Pharisees and other leaders of the Jews had made up their minds Jesus was a false teacher, perhaps because He had not attended "their schools."

d. Can we really argue with facts? Facts are stubborn things. The man insisted he could see. That was all the proof he needed. What would it take for others to see Jesus today?

8. "Finally, by the end of the story, we see that the formerly blind man is the only one who is truly seeing." https://www.missionadelante.org/blog/shannonjohn9.
What will it take for us to see Jesus as He was and how He is?

THOMAS

Zack Martin

FOCUS PASSAGE

John 20:24-31

ONE MAIN THING

Encountering the gospel does not do away with every doubt, grief, and disappointment. Still, it leads to being a wholly devoted, truth-seeking follower of Christ whom the sympathizing high priest, our elder brother, constantly aids. This is Thomas's story.

INTRODUCTION

Although Thomas was one of the original twelve (Matt 10:3, Mark 3:18, Luke 6:15, Acts 1:13), we know very little about him. Yet, his name itself gives us some interesting information about him. In Hebrew, the name Thomas means "a twin." The Greek equivalent is Didymus (John 11:16).[1] However, there is so much more to Thomas.

The three main passages that feature Thomas are found in the Gospel of John. Although our central passage is John 20:24–31, I think it would be a disservice to study it without knowing the full story of Thomas's faith journey. Thomas was much more than a doubter. His encounter with Jesus changed his life in ways that probably came as a surprise to him. Encountering the gospel will do the same for you as well. You may be more like Thomas than you know.

The first time Thomas had an active role in Scripture is in John 11. At this time, Jesus's reputation had spread far and wide, and even Samaritans had begun to believe in Jesus. However, He was rejected by a majority of Jewish religious elites. John 8:59 says that the Jews "picked up stones to throw at him, but Jesus hid himself and went out of the temple."[2] For this reason, He stayed on the other side of the Jordan River (John 10:40–42). Nevertheless, even there, He was succeeding, for many people were coming out to see and believe in Him.

While Jesus was staying on the other side of the Jordan, He heard that His best friend had become seriously ill. That friend would be Lazarus of Bethany, the brother of Martha and Mary. Jesus loved this family and loved being in their home. Yet, they lived about two miles southeast of Jerusalem at the bottom of the mountain (John 11:18). What would He do? He stayed where He was because He knew "this illness does not lead to death. It is for the glory of God, so that the Son of God may be glorified through it" (John 11:4).

However, Lazarus died; yet Jesus reassured His disciples that he only slept and delayed going to Bethany another two days. So, when the delay was over, Jesus said, "Let us go to him" (v 15). When Jesus gave the marching orders, everyone knew they were entering into a hostile environment, but Thomas spoke up with great courage, saying, "Let us also go, that we may die with him" (v 16).

Thomas showed undying devotion in this moment. He was wholly devoted to Christ, even to the point of death. What an example to follow! Furthermore, he even encouraged the other disciples to follow suit! Look at the text again (John 11:16); he said, "Let us," including the other disciples. His call was for all followers to be wholly devoted to Christ, even to the point of death. Is this not a sign of a true believer? One willing to give up everything, even his own life, to follow Jesus? Thomas was indeed a true believer.[3]

The second time that Thomas spoke up is in John 14:1–6. Jesus and His disciples were in an upper room celebrating their last Passover together. Here, Jesus gave parting words to His disciples because He would soon be betrayed, tried, and crucified. Jesus told them that He was about to leave them but that He would come again. While He was gone, He would be preparing a place for them, and when the time was right, He would come again and take them back with Him.

Jesus told His disciples they knew the way. Well, Thomas, the wholly devoted follower of Christ, was puzzled. Thomas spoke up because he wanted to go wherever Jesus was, but he did not know the way; at least, he thought he did not (John 14:4–5). As Lockyer explains, Thomas was not satisfied with his ignorance—and was not ashamed to show it.[4] And Jesus answered him. In John 14:6, Jesus said He was (and is) "the way, the truth, and the life."

GOING DEEPER

Now to our central passage. John 20:24–31 may be the only text you know anything about Thomas. This text influences the nickname "Doubting" Thomas. Setting Thomas apart makes him seem different than the other disciples both at that moment and today.[5] But I hope you now see Thomas as a wholly devoted follower of Jesus who was not ashamed of showing his ignorance. Those traits are brought with him to this text.

Jesus was crucified, buried, and raised on the third day. He then appeared to His disciples, but Thomas was not there. Can you imagine how that must have been for the disciples? What joy! Their Savior, who they thought was dead, buried, and gone forever, had now come back! The other disciples were so excited to share this good news with Thomas.

Why Thomas was not with them is only speculation. Some think that his sorrow was more significant than the others', and that is why he was missing.[6] This is likely to show that Thomas was wholly devoted to Christ even to the point of death, and he was assured that they knew where Jesus was going. So, it is not shocking that he was alone grieving, and it is not surprising that he wanted to experience what they experienced. This is why he told the others that he must physically touch the wounds of Jesus or else be unbelieving (John 20:25).

Then, eight days later, Thomas experienced what the other disciples had. He saw Jesus! Furthermore, Jesus repeated what Thomas expected out of that meeting. What a joy that Jesus hears us, even in our grief, disappointments, and doubt.[7] Thomas was beside himself. He no longer had doubt. He had been given everything he needed to believe, resulting in "the highest confession of Jesus' divinity in all the New Testament."[8]

Whether Thomas physically touched the wounds of Jesus is unknown, but what is known is that he came to have a deeper faith, which confessed Jesus to be God and that he worshipped Jesus. His life was forever changed! Thus, Jesus made Thomas a witness not only for the first century but also a witness for centuries to come because people will come to believe in Jesus based on Thomas's first-hand experience, which is recorded in Scripture. Those whose belief in Jesus is based on first-hand accounts from Thomas and the other disciples are more blessed (John 20:29).[9]

APPLICATION

I hope you have seen more to Thomas than just his moment of doubt after the resurrection of Jesus Christ in John 20:24–29. I hope you have seen yourself in Thomas and a desire to be more like him. How can you be more like him? First, you must be wholly devoted to Christ. There is no such thing as a half-hearted Christian. Total commitment is something that a Christian strives for from the beginning. In Luke 9:57–62, Jesus says that the cost of following Him means giving up things you hold dear in your life, which could include the comforts of this life, priorities of this life, and family.

Furthermore, once you start following Christ, you cannot look back. In the same chapter (Luke 9:23–27), Jesus says that followingHim will not be easy; not only will it cost you, but you must also take up your cross daily. Thomas was willing to die with Christ. Are you?

Second, Thomas was honest about his ignorance. Humility is a part of the Christian's character. We are told to emulate this specific character of Christ (Phil 2:1–11). Christians are told to put on humility with other characteristics (Col 3:12). So many Christians show their pride by being unteachable. Not wanting to be seen as ignorant is prideful. Be like Thomas and ask for help.

Third, Christians will have disappointments, grief, and doubt throughout their journey. It is important to remember that doubt is not a sin. While doubt is brought about by various circumstances and events, Christians need to remember that we have a great high priest who can sympathize with us, hear and care, and respond to us in our moments of weakness (Heb 4:14–16). Don't stop believing! Keep holding on to the anchor of one's soul! Keep confessing that Jesus is Lord!

CONCLUSION

Stand up, stand up for Jesus,
Stand in His strength alone;
The arm of flesh will fail you,
Ye dare not trust your own.
Put on the gospel armor,
Each piece put on with prayer;
Where duty calls, or danger,
Be never wanting there.

George Duffied, Jr.
"Stand Up, Stand Up for Jesus," 1858

DISCUSSION

1. Thomas had an undying devotion to Christ. He was willing to die and to go wherever Jesus was going. All Christians are called to have that same commitment to Christ. What is Jesus calling you to give up and what crosses are you called to bear in order to be His disciple?

2. Doubt is not a sin. Neither is faith blind. How is it that we can address these issues with people who allow their doubts to keep them from being a Christian?

ENDNOTES

[1] Herbert Lockyer, "Thomas," *All the Men of the Bible* (Grand Rapids: Zondervan, 1958), 527.

[2] Unless otherwise specified, all Bible references in this chapter are from the English Standard Version (ESV) (Wheaton: Crossway, 2016).

[3] Herbert, Lockyer, "Thomas," *All the Apostles of the Bible* (Grand Rapids: Zondervan, 1972), 176–178.

[4] Herbert Lockyer, *All the Men of the Bible*, 327.

[5] John MacArthur, *Twelve Ordinary Men* (Nashville: Thomas Nelson, 2002), 162–164.

[6] MacArthur, 163.

[7] D. A. Carson, *The Gospel According to John*, The Pillar New Testament Commentary (Grand Rapids: Eerdmans, 1991), 657.

[8] Beauford H. Bryant and Mark S. Krause, *John,* The College Press NIV Commentary (Joplin, MO: College Press, 1998), 400.

[9] Tradition says that Thomas was a missionary in India and was martyred for his faith there.

PENTECOST

Baron Vander Maas

FOCUS PASSAGE

Acts 1–2

Goal: The Gospel of Jesus Christ is universal. Luke, echoing images from the Old Testament, uses the miracle of speaking in tongues as a way that God unites people under his Kingdom. The day of Pentecost demonstrates the uniting force of the Gospel across nations, ethnicities, and languages.

INTRODUCTION

Very few times do we see the world united. Even as I am writing this in the year 2023, Russia and Ukraine are in constant war with each other. Israel and Palestine continue to fight due to terror attacks by Hamas. And the geopolitical climate of the United States and China is still very tense. But the world does in fact unify every other year for a series of different sporting events, also known as the Olympics. Every two years, interchanging between the summer and winter, the world gathers for approximately sixteen days to cheer and compete in a series of different sports.

In 2018, while the Olympics were held in Pyeong-Chang, South Korea, North and South Korea decided to merge and compete as one unified country. This was amid rising tensions and fear of North Korean retaliation on the US or South Korea. Forming the two countries together was meant to lead to some sense of unity.[1] Though it was inspiring and encouraging to see a moment of great unity, it did not last long. North and South Koreans did not dismantle the Demilitarized Zone, nor did they change their name to "Korea." However, it still provided a glimmer of hope for the possibility of humans working together. Above the efforts of mere men, the gospel's greatest ability is to unite people under King Jesus. Demonstrated on the day of Pentecost, the Gospel brings unity to people of different nationalities and countries through the power of God and his Spirit.

DIGGING DEEPER

The day of Pentecost, like many of the narratives within the New Testament, is recounted through the lens of an interpreter. By the power of the Spirit and the work of a dedicated writer, Luke shares God's purposes and will.[2] Luke gives theological meaning to church history in the way he describes certain details. While the day of Pentecost is a wonderful story itself, Luke highlights specific details that echo the Scriptures found in the Old Testament. Not only does he reveal the fulfillment of Old Testament prophecy, but also the work of God through true historical events. Here are three examples in which Luke fulfills Old Testament prophecy and alludes to some of its images.

One example is the reversal of the Tower of Babel story (Gen. 11:1–9). In this story, the early humans gather to "build a city, with a tower that reaches to the heavens..." (11:4). They plan to make a name for themselves. The Lord, against their idea, confuses their language and hinders them from understanding one another. In Acts, the apostles, filled with the Holy Spirit, are given the power to speak to one another in other tongues (Acts 2:4). This allows the many nations listed from verses 8–12 to understand them and Peter's sermon. While the Tower of Babel divides because of tongues, Pentecost brings unity with tongues. God reveals a picture of unity with the Gospel, as opposed to the loneliness and division that is demonstrated in Genesis through different languages (Gen 11:8–9; Acts 2:42–47).[3]

The second example is that of the theophany at Mt. Sinai (Exod 19:16–19).[4] Sinai is the beginning of the covenant between God and the Israelites. God dwells on the mountain in fire, wind, and storm. This event, obviously, is quite terrifying (Exod 19:16). How would you feel caught up in the middle of a lightning and thunderstorm? However, the demonstration and magnitude of God's presence via fire and storm are consistent in many Old Testament narratives, such as with Job (Job 38:1) or Solomon building the Temple (1 Kgs 8:10–11). At Pentecost, the apostles feel the same extraordinary force as that of Sinai. The apostles encounter God's presence through a "mighty rushing wind" from heaven and "divided tongues as of fire" in Acts 2. Luke wants us to encounter the Lord just like the Israelites. And just like the Israelites, the Lord has much in store for the church for many years to come. Pentecost is only the beginning!

The third example is the gathering of the nations in Isaiah 2:2–4.[5] In this stunning picture, Isaiah envisions a future world where all the nations are before God on Mt. Zion. These nations learn God's law and find peace among one another. The nations all become farmers; seeing that they no longer need swords or spears, their instruments of war become farming equipment (v. 4). Acts 2 is set in Jerusalem where the nations come together (calling by name each nation present), and those who are baptized create a community (Acts 2:42–47). It isn't a community of individual people with individual ideas and belongings, but a community that now shares, fellowships, and worships in the temple daily before our Lord.

In all these echoes, Luke purposefully highlights the different nations that met and were baptized on this holiday. It was God's wish to enter a covenant with a new people for the intended purpose of changing the world. That is the entire world rather than just a small subsection of it. God's plan is to unite the world together under His rule and law, and using the gift of tongues in Acts 2, He will bring the world under Christ.

APPLICATION

How often do people encounter someone who speaks a different language than their own native tongue? Like the ancient world, there are still many different languages and nationalities. You may have a Spanish-speaking customer at your work who needs help. Or perhaps a new immigrant family is moving into town and is learning the difficulty of

English. But language is not the only barrier towards communication, nor the only thing that we have that divides us!
What about the communication between different generations? A WWII veteran and a high schooler in 2023 are not
always going to communicate effectively. What about the
differences between the sexes? Men and women think differently and worry about different things. I do not know about
you, but my wife and I need help communicating every once
in a while (mainly my fault, not hers). Elders do not always
communicate openly or clearly about plans. Christians do not
always communicate hurt or purposes well. Good communication is a sign leading to unity, friendship, and even love.
When relationships lose communication, division increases.

The day of Pentecost illustrates God's ability to unite
people through the act of speaking in tongues. By giving
the apostles the Spirit to communicate over many
languages, we see the Gospel as universal, meant for all
nations. Notice Luke deliberately provides a list of all the
nations in attendance! So many different languages,
cultures, and people, but they all hear the gospel of Jesus
Christ (2:29–35). Three thousand are cut to the heart
because of Peter's illumination of their sin. Just like them,
we all hear the same gospel, we all feel the same regret for
our sins, and we all wish to be one in the same Father (Eph
4:4–6). The gospel is not only for the ancient world, but
also for the present world, and the world to come.

In today's culture, we want our differences to shine.
Diversity has become a buzzword meant ironically to unify
us. If everyone has differences, there is nothing different
about anyone. As a result, we focus only on our differences
and where we disagree. This phenomenon proves Jesus's
point that a house divided truly cannot stand, whether in
the world or the church (Mark 3:24–25). The Gospel puts

us all on the same playing field. It causes us to speak the same language. All have sinned and fallen short of God's glory, and all desperately need to be saved. Paul wants us to unite and ignore our differences, interestingly enough because of our baptism (Gal 3:26–27, Acts 2:38). Acts 2 becomes a reminder that God helps us speak together and that we all should listen attentively to what he has to say to us.

What can we do to encounter the uniting power of God? Many of us speak English, but sometimes we do not speak the same things! How can we solve this problem?

Understand human frailty in the face of sin. Peter's sermon is a confrontation with the sin of humanity. Those in attendance on Pentecost hanged Christ on the cross. However, we have all sinned against the Father. The gospel shows the deep and terrible power of sin, and how far it has reached into the human heart. Yet Christ's resurrection is the power of God for salvation (Acts 2:24, 32–35). Timothy Keller says it like this:

> The gospel is this: We are more sinful and flawed in ourselves than we ever dared believe, yet at the very same time we are more loved and accepted in Jesus Christ than we ever dared hope.[6]

As we share the gospel, we recognize our sin and frailty and God's desire to raise the dead to life. Just as the coin was lost amongst the couch cushions and the sheep within the trees, we also need to be saved. What a great day it is when a soul defeats the power of sin by the power of God!

Remember Jesus's mercy. Peter does not turn anyone away. While it would be easy to shut the door and keep the gospel away from sinners, it would not show the truth of

God's desire to save humanity (John 3:16). Rather, Peter shows the generous gift of salvation through baptism. The Lord has poured out His Spirit on the disciples as He promised by the prophet Joel (2:16–21), and He now wants to pour that same Spirit on those who give their lives to Him through faithfulness, repentance, and baptism (Acts 2:38). This is the free gift of God offered universally. We may be inclined to withhold such a great gift, but fortunately it is not ours to gatekeep or guard. May we always have the love of God to share the gospel with the weak, the poor, and the perishing.

Look for signs of God's uniting power. When Luke tells us the aftermath of the special event at Pentecost, it is not doom and gloom. People do not begin clawing at each other to get into heaven or argue about whose baptism was more correct. They eat together, they worship, they share, and they find peace in the community of God's love. This is an obvious expression of the type of unity God wants in His people. But so often in our churches, people find things to argue about. Instead of seeking after differences, let us glory in what makes us one in Christ our Savior. Let people truly know us by our love and genuine care (John 13:35).

DISCUSSION QUESTIONS

1. In what ways do you see congregations of the Lord's church struggling to unify? In what ways would finding a common language between people be helpful in fixing the problems?

2. What are some key features in Peter's sermon that you believe are worth remembering?

3. Looking at the church in Acts 2:42–47, what are some key characteristics of a thriving congregation? How are these characteristics an example of unification?

ENDNOTES

[1] Choe Sang-Hun, "North and South Korean Teams to March as One at Olympics" (*New York Times*, Jan 17, 2018).

[2] Carl R. Holladay, *Acts: A Commentary*, NTL (Louisville: WJK, 2016), 48–49.

[3] For more on the universal nature of the Gospel through the speaking in tongues see Eckard J. Schnabel, *Acts*, ZECNT (Grand Rapids: Zondervan, 2012), 123–25.

[4] For more information on fire and wind in the book of Acts during the day of Pentecost see Craig S. Keener, *Acts: An Exegetical Commentary* (Grand Rapids: Baker Academic, 2012), 1:801–02.

[5] See also Mark Moore, *Acts,* The College Press NIV Commentary (Joplin: College Press, 2011), 69–72. Moore references Isaiah 11:11–12 and sees the day of Pentecost as a return of the exiles from captivity.

[6] Timothy Keller, *The Meaning of Marriage* (Penguin: New York, 2011), 44.

12

THE UNIVERSAL REACH OF CHRISTIANITY

The Ethiopian

Robert L. Mann

FOCUS PASSAGE

Acts 8:26–40

ONE MAIN THING

The message of Jesus transcends cultural and geographical boundaries.

INTRODUCTION

In Acts 8:26–40, we have the story of an Ethiopian eunuch being led to the faith of Christ. Through God's providence, Philip is directed by an angel to meet the Ethiopian eunuch on a desert road that leads from Jerusalem to Gaza. The eunuch has traveled a great distance from Ethiopia to Jerusalem to worship but is struggling to understand the scroll of Isaiah. Philip is guided to the eunuch's chariot to explain how the scripture in Isaiah relates to Jesus as the Messiah, and he baptizes the eunuch. The eunuch continues his long journey to Ethiopia, rejoicing, and the Spirit of the Lord miraculously snatches away Philip.

GOING DEEPER

Philip the evangelist appears several times in the Acts of the Apostles. He was appointed as one of the seven men of good reputation, full of faith, wisdom, and the Holy Spirit, to help address the murmuring about neglecting the Greek-speaking Jewish widows in the daily food distribution by the Aramaic-speaking Jews as the number of disciples multiplied. They were tasked to serve the Grecian widows neglected in the daily administration. The Apostles' approach provided the means for them to continue the word of God while the disciples waited on tables. The method used to select disciples to serve the whole community pleased the multitude (Acts 6:1–6).

The seven disciples in Acts 6 hold no ecclesiastical office and are not to be mistaken as the first deacons by later traditions in the church. They did not hold formal offices in the household of God per the qualifications and qualities of a deacon as written in 1 Timothy 3:8–13. The number of the disciples was growing, and complaints arose concerning the mistreatment of Christian widows who were Greek-speaking Jews. There was a particular need to serve the widows who were being neglected because of their differences in their native language.

The Ethiopian eunuch was a quality person and considered a great man in his own country. His literacy and wealth are signified by having a chariot for transportation and possessing a scroll of Isaiah. He was trustworthy and in charge of all the queen's treasure. He possessed great authority as a high-ranking official in the court of Queen Candace. Still, he needed a sound preacher who could ignore their physical differences to explain the Scriptures and allow the word to transcend cultural and geographical boundaries. As people, we may find ourselves placing our mortal limits where God has no limits. We must always be mindful that the reach of God's word is universal and is for every human on the planet.

The Ethiopian descriptor of the eunuch refers to the color of his skin and being a descendant of Ham, where "Cush" refers to Ethiopia (Gen 10:6). Cush traditionally refers to the region south of Egypt, referred to as Ethiopia by classical authors. Eunuchs had limitations placed on their spiritual lives. They were not permitted to become full Jewish proselytes. Instead, the eunuch could become a "God-fearer" (Deut 23:1).

Although the Ethiopian eunuch was a "God-fearer" like many are today, he was still lost. The Ethiopian eunuch studied and worshipped but was dead in sin, without Christ, and afar from God. The Ethiopian eunuch was far from home and concerned about his spiritual life. The baptism of an Ethiopian eunuch breaks social and ritual barriers. The educated eunuch needed a preacher to explain that Jesus is the Messiah and that baptism for the remission of sins is required to become a Christian.

APPLICATION

The text shows how the Spirit guided Philip to join the eunuch on his chariot to teach Jesus to a stranger with a soul to be saved. God opens doors of opportunity in unlikely places, even on a desert road, where probabilities may be remote to share the word of God. This lesson teaches us always to be ready to share the gospel with everyone. In this lesson, we can see that those who gladly received His word were baptized on the day of Pentecost (Acts 2:41).

The Ethiopian was a foreigner, and not everyone reaches out spiritually to those of different cultures and geographical boundaries, yet the gospel and divine grace notice everyone. There are many groups of people world-wide, and it is wrong to share the gospel only with those with similarities. Philip was ready to do the work of the Lord. God wills that all men be saved and know the truth (1 Tim 2:4).

Philip explained the passage from Isaiah and connected the same Scripture to Jesus as the Messiah. Although inferred, Philip spoke of the essential act of baptism in water for the remission of sin. This truth of water baptism is proven as the eunuch saw water and asked what hindered him from being baptized. The eunuch also had to believe that Christ was the Messiah. Philip's statement, "If you believe with all your heart, thou mayest," proves this truth. The eunuch answered and said I believe that Jesus is the Son of God. The eunuch commanded the chariot to stop, and they both went down in the water, and the eunuch was baptized.

Although the eunuch had the mental capacity required to be the queen's treasurer and the prestige to have his chariot driver, he didn't understand the meaning of the prophetic text that spoke of the suffering and sacrifice of the Messiah. Not all who read the scriptures will compre-hend without an explanation. Although intelligent and with great authority, the eunuch needed some guidance to help comprehend the Scriptures. Here, we learn to study the Bible to share the meaning of the text with others. We

understand the value of sitting down with someone and
meeting them where they are in their spiritual journey. We
see that Jesus Christ and water baptism coexist for salvation. "Then Peter said unto them, Repent and be baptized
every one of you in the name of Jesus Christ for the remission of sins, and ye shall receive the gift of the Holy
Ghost" (Acts 2:38).

CONCLUSION

Our text teaches about a significant encounter between
Philip and the Ethiopian eunuch. The two men came from
vastly different cultures and geographical boundaries, but
the message of Jesus has the power to transcend all things
that separate humankind. God does not allow cultural and
geographical differences to hinder one from being added
to the body of Christ. "For by one Spirit are we all
baptized into one body, whether we be Jew or Gentiles,
whether we be bond or free; and have been all made to
drink into one Spirit" (1 Cor 12:13). God sees differently
than us: "There is neither Jew nor Greek, there is neither
bond nor free, there is neither male nor female: for ye are
all one in Christ Jesus" (Gal 3:28).

The Ethiopian eunuch displayed humility by admitting
he did not understand his reading. We learn the important
lesson of the continuous journey of learning the Scriptures. There are times when we will need someone to
guide us to a better understanding of God's word. Let us
be encouraged to dive deeper into the Bible so that we
may show someone who is struggling how to comprehend
the Scriptures.

Philip was prepared to faithfully follow the Lord's
instructions to meet with the Ethiopian eunuch in a place

that most would consider unlikely to baptize someone. He trusted in the Lord and was obedient to God's word. We should strive to do the same as Philip and remain ready to share the gospel that transcends all cultural and geographical differences for Christ's will.

Philip's Greek background proved an excellent immediate choice for serving the community of widows discriminated against in the church. His background consisted of being an obedient personal worker and a faithful preacher. He preached Christ the Messiah and performed miracles in Samaria (Acts 8:5–6). Philip had gained experience in dealing with language and cultural differences. He was prepared to reach beyond the walls of being different.

Philip had the attitude of the shepherd, similar to the parable of the lost sheep (Matt 18:10–14). Jesus shows that the kingdom is accessible to all sinners who have gone astray from God. He was instrumental in the early spread of Christianity across cultures. He transcended geographical boundaries by proclaiming the good news to the eunuch and baptized him into Jesus Christ.

DISCUSSION QUESTIONS

1. Are you humble enough to admit there are scriptures you do not understand?
2. What can one do to improve his or her understanding of the scriptures?
3. Do you share the gospel in ways that help transcend cultural and geographical boundaries?
4. Are you hesitant to share the gospel with someone who looks different?

13

THE PHILOSOPHERS OF ATHENS

Jeremy Barrier

Sometimes an encounter with the message of Jesus is...unfamiliar, even destabilizing and unpredictable! Such was the case in Acts 17. This type of presentation is what is both exciting and terrifying about sharing good news. You simply don't know how people will react to you!

FOCUS PASSAGE

Acts 17:16–34 (KJV)

> Now while Paul waited for them at Athens, his spirit was stirred in him, when he saw the city wholly given to idolatry. Therefore disputed he in the synagogue with the Jews, and with the devout persons, and in the market daily with them that met with him. Then certain philosophers of the Epicureans, and of the Stoicks, encountered him. And some said, What will this babbler say? other some, He seemeth to be a setter forth of strange gods: because he preached unto them Jesus, and the resurrection. And they took him, and brought him unto Areopa-

gus, saying, May we know what this new doctrine, whereof thou speakest, is? For thou bringest certain strange things to our ears: we would know therefore what these things mean. (For all the Athenians and strangers which were there spent their time in nothing else, but either to tell, or to hear some new thing.) Then Paul stood in the midst of Mars' hill, and said, Ye men of Athens, I perceive that in all things ye are too superstitious. For as I passed by, and beheld your devotions, I found an altar with this inscription, To The Unknown God. Whom therefore ye ignorantly worship, him declare I unto you. God that made the world and all things therein, seeing that he is Lord of heaven and earth, dwelleth not in temples made with hands; Neither is worshipped with men's hands, as though he needed any thing, seeing he giveth to all life, and breath, and all things; And hath made of one blood all nations of men for to dwell on all the face of the earth, and hath determined the times before appointed, and the bounds of their habitation; That they should seek the Lord, if haply they might feel after him, and find him, though he be not far from every one of us: For in him we live, and move, and have our being; as certain also of your own poets have said, For we are also his offspring. Forasmuch then as we are the offspring of God, we ought not to think that the Godhead is like unto gold, or silver, or stone, graven by art and man's device. And the times of this ignorance God winked at; but now commandeth all men every where to repent: Because he hath appointed a day, in the which he will judge the world in righteousness by that man whom he hath ordained; whereof he hath given assurance unto all men, in that he hath raised him from the dead. And when they heard of the resurrection of the

dead, some mocked: and others said, We will hear thee
again of this matter. So Paul departed from among them.
Howbeit certain men clave unto him, and believed:
among the which was Dionysius the Areopagite, and a
woman named Damaris, and others with them.

ONE MAIN THING

Allow God's Spirit to be Stirred

INTRODUCTION

A few years ago, I was in New Delhi, India. What an
amazing city! With over 32 million inhabitants in the
metro area, this makes Delhi the second largest
metropolitan area on planet Earth. One would be hard-
pressed to find a city that is more diverse with religions
equally represented than anywhere else on the planet.
While there, we always spend time with our loving
coworkers in the faith, whom I have known for three
decades now! However, in addition to this, there is always
time to visit, for instance, the Jama Masjid—one of the
largest mosques in the world built by the Mughal emperor
Shah Jahan almost four hundred years ago—or any number
of Hindu temples! Again, an amazing place! At any rate,
after a *huge dinner of fried chicken specifically tailored to our
North American, southern standards* at the home of Sunny
and Nargis David, we decided to step outside for a walk
around the neighborhood to "walk off" the meal. Within
moments we were standing outside a community Hindu
temple. I was with my brother Joey, and one other
colleague, Travis, whom I nudged on the shoulder and said,
"Hey, let's check out the temple!" As was a typical custom,

we respectfully walked around the temple noting the gods, people praying, incense, and numerous other fascinating aspects of a temple, when suddenly I was tapped on the shoulder. I turned around. An angry man was within inches of my face, scowling at me, and looking as if he were on the edge of doing us some real harm! I gently responded to his tap by stating "Yes, may I help you?" He didn't waste any time. "Get out! You have no business being in this temple! This temple is for Hindus!"

In moments like this, one doesn't quite have time to think correctly, and often times we do something that is called a *reaction*. Yes, I reacted, and an argument ensued. The reason I mention this story—to which I shall come back later—is due to several reasons. First, when variant religious beliefs or even different cultures meet, then sometimes there is a clash of ideas (or worse). This can be disconcerting and worrying. Second, in this particular moment, I will have to admit, my *spirit was stirred within me.*

GOING DEEPER

When we consider the account of Paul entering Athens— soon after his depressing departure from Thessalonica and Berea, and just before his exciting entrance into Corinth, we see the apostle Paul *stirred within his spirit.* To be clear, from a grammatical point of view, the text does not indicate whether this "stirring" is good or bad. It just is. To emphasize my point, this same Greek verb is used in only one other place in the New Testament, and that is 1 Corinthians 13:5, and in this context it is not a good thing: "love...is not provoked." In fact, the indications are that allowing oneself to be "urged on," "stimulated," "irritated," or "provoked" can have real downsides. Nevertheless, this is not inconsistent with Paul, and let's just say that regardless of the start of Acts 17:16, the rest is history. In Paul's case, his initial stirring allowed him to present the good news of God *in the synagogue*, and *in the marketplace* with other devout people, which inevitably led to a moment where people with different religious understandings of God were having a *real encounter!* How cool. I love these moments. In Paul's case, this initial stirring allowed him the opportunity to share his message at the heart of Athens, at the *Areopagus* no less, where many, who without a doubt, had never considered the resurrection of Jesus before were now being given the opportunity to think it through—and even respond in some cases!

APPLICATION

While I will be the first to admit that we have barely even scraped the surface of Acts 17, I have consolidated my thoughts to emphasize the initial activity of Paul ... to be stirred in his spirit. While, to be clear, this is not a stirring of the *Spirit* within Paul—the text is not clear, one can agree that this is a stirring of Paul as a person that *leads to a stirring of God's Spirit in Athens.* In other words, as Paul was able to proclaim the message of Jesus, this is without a doubt an opportunity for God's breath and Word to be presented to the Athenians in no small way. My concern for people today is that they are not "stirred," and in fact, their emotional selves are hardly even engaged in their faith! There is nothing more profound and real in our churches than a people who are stirred to do good things, because of the good news.

CONCLUSION

As I stood there in the Hindu temple in New Delhi, India, I'll be the first to admit that what I said afterward was hardly effective (according to my reckoning), although I was very sincere. I attempted to reason with the man. I tried this in several ways, yet nothing I said mattered. "Get out!" was the only message for us on that day. As we left the temple, and I explained how the God of the universe "dwells not in temples made with hands," I'll have to admit that Paul's ineffective message from 2,000 years ago in Athens worked no better in 2010. Either way, if there is anything that I hope remains from the encounter, it would be as follows: 1) we were peaceful people, 2) we were sincerely interested in their temple, 3) we were very sincere about our own faith, and 4) God doesn't dwell in temples! As you study the words of Acts 17, I hope that your faith is stirred. I hope that as you encounter the divine, it will lift your spirits and challenge your assumptions. Also, I hope it will cause you to be willing to encounter others with your faith! It is not always a "clash" of ideas, but sometimes it is a synergy of understanding. I have experienced this on many occasions as well. How encouraging to see people hear and understand!

DISCUSSION

1. When Paul entered Athens, his spirit was stirred. Is this a good thing or a bad thing?
2. Was Paul effective in sharing the message of God in his encounter with the Athenian philosophers?

3. Even if we are not immediately successful in sharing our ideas, should we stop sharing our ideas or ideas about our faith?

4. In the book of Acts, God *not* living in temples—whether Jewish or Greek—seems to be an important theme. Is this important even today?

FELIX

Acts 24

Bill Bagents

FOCUS PASSAGE

> But this I confess to you, that according to the Way,
> which they call a sect, I worship the God of our fathers,
> believing everything laid down by the Law and written in
> the Prophets, having a hope in God, which these men
> themselves accept, that there will be a resurrection of
> both the just and the unjust (Acts 24:14–15).

ONE MAIN THING

The gospel doesn't exist in a vacuum; it powerfully engages
past, present, and future.

INTRODUCTION

Following a false accusation and a vow by forty men "to
neither eat nor drink" until they had killed Paul (Acts
23:21), Roman commander Claudius Lysias had 200

soldiers whisk the apostle from Jerusalem to safety in Caesarea. Thus, Paul found himself on trial before the Roman governor Felix. The inconclusive trial morphed into a gospel encounter where both Felix and his wife, Druscilla, willingly heard Paul "speak about faith in Christ Jesus" (Acts 24:24).

GOING DEEPER

Paul's accusers wanted him dead. Tertullus described him to Felix as "a plague, one who stirs up riots among all the Jews throughout the world and is a ringleader of the sect of the Nazarenes. He even tried to profane the temple" (Acts 24:5–6). Their words may well have backfired. Rather than making Paul look sinister, for an official who was married to a Jewish lady (Acts 24:24) and who had "a rather accurate knowledge" of Christianity (Acts 24:22), these over-the-top accusations may have made Paul even more interesting to Felix and others. It's a classic dirty debate tactic—if you can't attack the message, attack the messenger. When it backfires, it tends to do so dramatically.

Paul's defense was simple and strategic. "They did not find me disputing with anyone or stirring up a crowd" (Acts 24:12). More importantly, "It is with respect to the resurrection of the dead that I am on trial before you this day" (Acts 24:21). To summarize, "They can't prove their civil case; their case isn't even civil. I am here because of the Way and the resurrection." Paul's defense wasn't about acquittal. For him, it was about faithfulness in his mission to bring the gospel to the entire Gentile world.

Felix was no saint. He heard enough to know the charges were—at best—exaggerated. Felix also wasn't the worst of men. Though he postponed a verdict, he had the centurion grant Paul "some liberty" and allow his friends to attend to his needs (Acts 24:23).

The text doesn't tell us why Felix (and Druscilla) "sent for Paul and heard him speak about faith in Christ Jesus" (Acts 24:24). To what degree was knowing about "the Way" of particular interest to Felix? Did Druscilla's ethnicity play a role? Was there any measure of genuine spiritual interest? Whatever the motive(s), for an evangelist to be asked to speak about faith is perfect.

The word "gospel" does not appear in Acts 24, but it is vividly described. "And as he reasoned about righteousness and self-control and the coming judgment, Felix was alarmed and said, 'Go away for the present. When I get an opportunity, I will summon you'" (Acts 24:25). Sadly, we also learn that Felix's motives were not pure: "At the same time he hoped some money would be given to him by Paul" (Acts 24:26). After a two-year delay, Felix was succeeded by Festus, "and desiring to do the Jews a favor, Felix left Paul in prison (Acts 24:27). We're never told whether Felix moved from fear to faith.

APPLICATION

We've always loved the sentiment attributed to the Roman philosopher Seneca: "Wherever there is a human being, there is an opportunity for kindness." Could there be a greater kindness than teaching someone about faith in Christ Jesus? Felix was a potential enemy of Paul—presumably he held the power of life and death over the apostle. But Paul didn't consider Felix an enemy. Paul saw the governor as a soul precious to God and in need of the gospel. For Paul, the trial and his freedom were never primary. The opportunity to present the gospel was the greater need and the chief focus. We love how the gospel opposes selfishness and puts both the King and the kingdom first (Matt 6:33, Phil 1:21–30).

We love how Paul framed his defense in terms of the resurrection. Since Felix knew about the Way, he would not have missed the gospel reference. Everything—all love, joy, hope, service, and sacrifice—rests on the fact of a resurrected Lord (1 Cor 15)! Because He rose, all will rise. Because He rose, the saints will rise to glory. Because He rose and all judgment has been committed to Him, all will be judged (2 Cor 5:9–11, John 5:22).

Paul strategically prepared his presentation of the gospel to Felix. Resurrection presents hope—there will be life after physical death. People had given their lives for the Way—think of Stephen (Acts 7), James the brother of John (Acts 12), and those Paul (as Saul) had helped kill (Acts 22:4, 26:10). If the Way was worth dying for, it was certainly worth learning about.

Of all people, a judge would understand authoritative judgment. As Paul "reasoned about righteousness and self-control and the coming judgment, Felix was alarmed ..." (Acts 24:25). Paul's presentation of the gospel hit a nerve. We infer that righteousness and self-control were not strengths. We infer that Felix had some degree of belief in God and some sense of right and wrong. We also infer that Paul tailored his presentation of the gospel to Felix's character and behavior. He targeted God's truth to reach the heart of his prospect.

Regrettably, some limit the content of the gospel to the death, burial, and resurrection of Jesus (1 Cor 15:1–8). Clearly, these are matters of "first importance." They succinctly describe the heart of the gospel. However, they neither oppose nor exclude the broader doctrine of Christ stressed in Matthew 28:18–20, Acts 2:42, Colossians 3:17, 1 Peter 4:11a, 2 John 9, and Jude 3.

To offer a supporting yet different perspective, when Philip told the Ethiopian treasurer "the good news about Jesus," the first question from the man was, "See here is water! What prevents me from being baptized?" (Acts 8:35–36) The preaching of the good news included instruction about baptism. Note how beautifully Acts 8:12 foreshadows Philip's encounter with the treasurer.

When Peter and Barnabas erred in withholding fellowship from Gentile brethren, Paul's description of the situation was, "When I saw that their conduct was not in step with the truth of the gospel ..." (Gal 2:14). Being in step with the gospel includes loving all the brethren and treating them like family.

In Acts 14:15, Paul and Barnabas brought the people of Lystra "good news that you should turn from these vain things to the living God." Just as Acts 24:25 strongly implies, the good news includes a message of repentance, of turning from sin and to God. Titus 2:11–15 enhances our understanding that the appearance of the grace of God in the person of Jesus trains us "to renounce ungodliness and worldly passions, and to live self-controlled, upright, and godly lives ...." It would be challenging to miss the resonance between Titus 2:12 and Acts 24:24–25!

The connection between the gospel and godly living is also enhanced by the three New Testament passages that speak of obeying the gospel (Rom 10:16, 2 Thess 1:8, and 1 Pet 4:17). It is beautifully clear in Philippians 1:27: "Only let your manner of life be worthy of the gospel of Christ ...."

When Paul reasoned with Felix "about righteousness and self-control and the coming judgment," he was doing just what the text states—he was speaking about "faith in Christ Jesus." He was preaching the gospel!

CONCLUSION

Felix's encounter with the gospel did not end well. He heard and believed enough to be alarmed, but not enough to act. Acts 24:26 offers one reason; he loved money more than being right with God. What a needed warning in our day!

Felix's words offer another strong warning—a warning about assumptions. "Go away for the present. When I get an opportunity, I will summon you" (Acts 24:25). Felix had his opportunity with Paul on that fateful day. The Bible is clear—he had no way to know he'd ever get another (Luke 12:16–21, Jas 4:13–17). He also had no assurance that his heart would not harden before a second gospel encounter. Neither do we.

DISCUSSION QUESTIONS

1. Are we correct in asserting that Paul saw every encounter as a potential gospel encounter? If so, why? If not, offer examples of the exceptions.
2. How do you account for Felix's "rather accurate knowledge of the Way"? What does that tell you about Felix? About the progress of the gospel?
3. Why would Felix send for Paul to hear "him speak about faith in Christ Jesus"? Do you think Felix had genuine interest in the gospel?

4. Why did Felix react to Paul's presentation of the gospel with fear?

5. Why did Felix send Paul away after his gospel message?

6. What should we make of the parting words of Felix, "Go away for the present. When I get an opportunity, I will summon you"? Were these words sincere or a dodge?

AGRIPPA

Acts 26

Wayne Kilpatrick

FOCUS PASSAGE

Acts 25:13—26:32

ONE MAIN THING

The purpose of this text is to give the account of Paul's appeal to Caesar, thus allowing him to travel to Rome and preach the gospel there. Paul was arrested under the Procurator (Governor) Felix, who was preparing to be replaced by Festus. "But after two years Porcius Festus came into Felix's room: and Felix, willing to show the Jews a pleasure, left Paul bound."[1] Paul was then left at the mercy of the judgment of Festus. Herod Agrippa II was allowed, by the gratitude of the Romans, to be king over parts of this region. Thus, he becomes a part of Paul's judgment.

INTRODUCTION

The old adage "Like father; like son" comes into play in this text; only here it is "like father; like children." Herod Agrippa II is the son of Herod Agrippa I, and Bernice is his daughter. Agrippa, the son, loved the pomp and pageantry that went along with his position as king. That was illustrated in Acts 12:21–23, KJV. Herod Agrippa I was eaten of worms after he made a speech and was called a god by the people of Tyre and Sidon. Herod did not rebuke them for calling him a god, so God sent an angel to smite him and he died, having been eaten of worms. Josephus the Jewish historian also gave an account of this event and revealed additional information.[2] In his account Josephus revealed that Herod Agrippa I, on that day, wore a garment made of silver and it glistened in the sun, thus inciting the people to call him a god. Herod Agrippa I's response or non-response was in contrast to Paul and Barnabas when the people at Lystra called them by the names of Roman gods. The two men immediately tore their robes and prevented the people from sacrificing to them.[3]

Like Herod Agrippa I, his children also loved the praises of men. Father and great-grandfather did not mind scandal; neither did Agrippa II and Bernice. The historian Josephus wrote that the constant companionship of Herod Agrippa II and his sister Bernice created a scandal.[4] Juvenal, a Roman poet active in the late first and early second century A.D., wrote of this scandal in his satire on (The Rich And Beautiful)—

> ... and some legendary diamond made the more precious
> by once gracing Berenice's finger, a gift to his incestuous

sister from Barbarous Herod Agrippa, a present for her, in far-off Judaea, where barefoot kings observe their day of rest on the Sabbath, And their tradition grants merciful indulgence to elderly pigs.[5]

As Juvenal had written: Herod II was barbarous and very immoral. Thus, he had a bad reputation among the Romans and Jews.

Agrippa II, the last king of the Herodian house, was reared in Rome at the court of Claudius and enjoyed this emperor's signal favor. Upon the death of his father Herod Agrippa I in 44, Claudius wanted to make the young prince, who was then seventeen years old, king in his father's place but met with general disapproval. For six additional years he was kept in Rome in order to learn Roman ways, then in 50 was given the Herodian principality of Chalcis on the Anti-Lebanons and gradually a much greater territory in northern and northwestern Palestine. As the ruler of the Temple, he had to become conversant with Judaism and adopt Jewish ways.[6] Like his great-grandfather, Herod the Great, and his father, he understood Judaism. Perhaps this was the reason he was involved with the Apostle Paul's case.

The stage for the drama of Agrippa's interaction with Paul began several days before Agrippa came to visit Caesarea. Paul had been arrested for his own safety in Jerusalem when mob violence threatened his life.[7] He was brought to Caesarea (the Roman capital of this province) to be judged by the governor, Felix. Felix was in transition and was about to be replaced by Porcius Festus as Governor. In order to show a favor to the Jews, Felix left Paul (yet unjudged) in prison. That is why Paul's case was brought in front of the new governor, who seemed to have little or no experience in these kinds of matters. When Festus called Paul before him and did not render a judgment, Paul appealed to Caesar, which was not expected by Festus.[8] F. F. Bruce commented on the implication of Paul's appeal to Caesar:

> Festus heard Paul's words with much relief. By appealing to Caesar, Paul enabled him to escape from a responsibility with which he felt unable to cope. He conferred with his council, a body consisting of the higher officials of his administration and younger men who accompanied him in order to gain some experience of provincial government—and willingly agreed that Paul's case should be referred to Rome, in fact, once Paul had made his appeal, Festus had no option in the matter.[9]

Due to Festus's inexperience, He had to speak with his council of legal advisors about this matter. After speaking with his council, he had no choice but to send Paul to Rome. His reply to Paul was: "Hast thou (or You have) appealed unto Caesar? unto Caesar shalt thou go."[10] Festus now had a problem. Despite the high airs projected by Festus in his courtroom, he was now placed in quite a quandary when Paul appealed to Caesar. When he sent Paul to Rome, (to have his case heard before the emperor), it would be necessary for him to send a report of the case as it had developed up to the moment of Paul's appeal. When Agrippa arrived a few days later, Festus must have felt a sense of relief. Agrippa, like his great-grandfather Herod the Great, had knowledge of the Jewish laws and customs. As the ruler of the Temple, he had to become conversant with Judaism and adopt Jewish ways.[11] No doubt Festus thought Agrippa would be able to advise him on the situation.

GOING DEEPER

Now enters Agrippa upon the scene.[12]

> Now some days having passed, Agrippa, the king, and Bernice went down to Caesarea saluting Festus. This visit was a formal greeting of the new procurator and hence was made so soon after his assumption of office. Agrippa had his capital in Caesarea Philippi (which he renamed Neronias in honor of Nero), north of the Sea of Galilee, and he came down from there to the procurator's capital Caesarea. One ruler honors and welcomes another into office. While Festus and Agrippa each had their own territory, given by the emperor, Claudius, Agrippa had received the rule over the Temple in Jerusalem and the privilege to appoint the high priests. This arrangement was still in force under Nero and naturally prompted a formal visit such as this.

Fortunately for Festus, a way out of this situation had just presented itself with the arrival of Herod Agrippa II.[13] This Herod Agrippa was the ruler of a small kingdom to the northeast of Festus's province. He had come to Caesarea, on a complimentary visit, to congratulate the new procurator on his appointment. This man was reputed to be an expert in Jewish religious questions, and Festus hoped he might give him some unofficial help in drafting his report. So, after many days had passed Festus, seemingly in a casual manner, brought up Paul's case to Agrippa. He summarized the details of the case against Paul.[14]

Agrippa agreed to hear the charges brought against Paul.[15] The next day Paul was allowed to speak before Agrippa and Festus in the courtroom.[16]

Paul began his speech by praising Agrippa for his expertise in the Jewish laws and customs, no doubt insinuating that Agrippa would be fair in his judgment toward him.[17] Paul gave a summary autobiography. He spoke of his youth, his education, his being a Pharisee, his devotedness to God, his conversion to Christianity, and his faith in the resurrection of Christ from the dead.[18] When he had finished speaking, Agrippa said to him: "Almost thou persuadest me to be a Christian."[19] Some scholars have debated whether Agrippa asked Paul a question with this statement or if he was truly saying: "You have almost persuaded me to become a Christian." Either way, there is nothing else given that shows Agrippa ever became a Christian. One of the saddest phrases ever to be uttered is "almost persuaded."

And when he had thus spoken, the king rose, and the governor, and Bernice, and they that sat with them.[20] Agrippa's rising signaled the hearing had ended.

APPLICATION

God uses wicked men to aid in the spreading of his work. In the case of Paul's trial, a pagan governor would not render a verdict, thus forcing Paul to appeal to Caesar's court. Agrippa, the morally bankrupt king who was technically recognized as a Jew, with his indecisiveness, reinforced Festus's decision to send Paul to Caesar's court in Rome. The ultimate result of these men's indecisiveness was that Paul could preach the gospel in Rome. When Paul appealed to Caesar, he turned the table on Festus. He had nothing to charge against Paul, thus there was no documentation to send to Rome explaining what charges had been brought against the prisoner. That was the situation that unsettled Festus. Agrippa was no help to Festus, so he was in a "fix." He would not dare set Paul free after he appealed to Caesar, for fear someone might report him to Caesar. We know Festus was in office for about three years. Agrippa was king until Jerusalem fell to the Romans in 70 A.D., thus ending the Jewish State.[21]

What do we learn from this study? One can readily see what indecisiveness can do. In Festus and Agrippa's cases, it caused an innocent man to suffer a horrible injustice. This, through God's providence, caused the spreading of the Gospel throughout Rome and the Italian provinces. We also learn that our plans can be turned around us, as they were on Festus when his actions forced Paul to appeal to Caesar's court. This brings to mind a famous quote of David Crockett's: "Be sure you are right then go ahead."[22] That is good advice for Christians in our time. Agrippa and Festus failed miserably in following that rule.

DISCUSSION QUESTIONS

1. What kind of name did Agrippa have among the Jews and the Romans? Discuss.
2. Is a good name important? Proverbs 22:1 (KJV) says "A good name is rather to be chosen than great riches, and loving favor rather than silver and gold." Ecclesiastes 7:1 adds "A good name is better than precious ointment; and the day of death than the day of one's birth."
3. What is God's providence?

4. What kind of defense did Paul use?
5. Is almost being persuaded a good thing? If yes, explain; if no, explain.
6. Festus had a council, but there is no indication of their advice to him in the matter of Paul. What could have caused this lack of revelation?

ENDNOTES

[1] Acts 24:27 KJV

[2] Josephus, *Antiquities*. XIX. 8, 2

[3] Acts 14:8–18

[4] Josephus, Antiquities. XX. 7. 3

[5] Juvenal, *Satire*. vi, 155

[6] Acts 26:2–3

[7] Acts 21:33

[8] Acts 25:10–11

[9] F. F. Bruce, *The Book Of Acts*, Rev. ed. (Grand Rapids, MI: Eerdmans, 1988).

[10] Acts 25:10–11

[11] Acts: 26:2–3

[12] Acts 25:13–22

[13] Acts 25:13

[14] Acts 25:14–22

[15] Acts 25:22

[16] Acts 26:1–27

[17] Acts 26:2–3

[18] Acts 26:1–26

[19] Acts 26:28

[20] Acts 26:30

[21] Josephus, *Antiquities*. XX.173–184

[22] Carved on David Crockett's monument on the old courthouse square in Lawrenceburg, Tennessee.

Scripture Index

Old Testament
Genesis
3:15	ix
10:6	92
11:1‒9	84
11:4	84
11:8‒9	84
12	7
12:1‒3	6
12:3	ix
22	7
22:18	4
39:9	20

Exodus
19:16	84
19:16‒19	84
40:34	9

Leviticus
20:10	64

Numbers
15:32‒36	59

Deuteronomy
17:6‒7	59‒60
18:15‒22	ix
19:16‒18	40
22:22‒27	64

23:1	92

1 Kings
8:10‒11	84
17:8‒24	3, 7

2 Chronicles
7:1‒3	9
16:9	13

Job
38:1	84

Psalms
51:4	20
145:1‒7	12‒13

Proverbs
22:1	116

Ecclesiastes
7:1	116

Isaiah
2:2‒4	85
2:4	85
9:6	ix
11:11‒12	89
53	x
53:2	x
53:3‒4	x

Daniel
6:9‒14	21

7	19	4:32	17
7:13–14	19	4:36	17
Hosea		5	17, 19
6:6	65	5:17–26	15–16, 65
Joel		5:20	18
2:16–21	88	5:24	18
		6:15	74
New Testament		7	23
Matthew		7:1–10	23
6:33	106	7:11–17	23
8:20	18–19	7:18–35	23
9:1–8	65	7:36	23
9:13	65	7:36–37	23
10:3	74	7:36–50	22–23, 65
12:7	65	7:37	23
18:10–14	95	7:39	23–25
23:23	65	7:39–40	26
25:31–46	65	7:40–43	24
26:64	19	7:42	25
26:64–68	21	7:47	25–27
28:18–20	107	7:47–48	26
Mark		7:48	27
2:1–12	65	7:48–50	25
2:4	18	7:49	23, 27
3:8	5	7:50	26
3:18	74	9:23–27	78
3:24–25	86	9:45	31
7	2, 7	9:57–62	78
7:1–23	3	12:16–21	108
7:24–30	1–3	15:1	23
7:25	4	16:31	34
7:26–29	3	19:10	26, 50
7:27	5	21:38	63
10:17	44	24:9	31
10:23	44	24:13	30
Luke		24:13–35	29–30,
2:8–20	8	33–34	
2:11	22	24:15–16	31
2:12	10	24:16	37
2:19	11	24:39	35
2:38	23	24:41–43	35
4:25–26	3	24:53	63
4:26	17	**John**	

1:11	x	7:50⁻52	44⁻45
1:12	x	7:53⁻8:11	55⁻56,
1:12⁻13	43	58, 62⁻63	
1:19	41	8:59	75
1:25⁻26	42	9	67
1:29⁻34	42	9:2	67
1:32	43	9:3⁻5	68
1:34	43	9:8⁻12	69
2:1⁻12	41	9:18⁻19	70
2:13⁻23	41	9:18⁻23	70
2:23	41	9:24	70
2:24⁻25	24	9:33	71
3	41, 43⁻44	9:35⁻39	72
3:1	40	9:40⁻41	72
3:1⁻9	45	10:40⁻42	75
3:1⁻15	38	11	75
3:2	40	11:4	75
3:3	44	11:15	75
3:4	42	11:16	74, 76
3:5	42	11:18	75
3:9	41	12:23	19
3:16	43, 88	13:35	88
3:22	42	14:1⁻6	76
3:34	43	14:4⁻5	76
4:1⁻21	48	14:6	xi, 45, 76
4:4	49	16:8⁻11	65
4:16⁻18	50⁻51	18:31⁻32	64
4:24	51	19:38⁻42	45
4:28⁻29	53	20:16	32
4:34	53	20:19	35
4:39	53	20:24⁻29	78
5:22	106	20:24⁻31	74⁻75, 77
5:27	65	20:25	77
6	44	20:26	35
6:60	44	20:29	78
6:63	43	20:30⁻31	32
6:66	44	21:25	41, 63
7	39	**Acts**	
7:36	63	1⁻2	82
7:45⁻46	40	1:8	22
7:49	40	1:13	74
7:50	40	2	84⁻85, 87
7:50⁻51	46	2:4	84

2:8–12	84	25:14–22	117
2:24	87	25:22	117
2:29–35	86	26	109
2:32–35	87	26:1–26	117
2:38	87–88, 94	26:1–27	117
2:41	93	26:2–3	117
2:42	107	26:10	106
2:42–47	84–85, 89	26:18	xi
6	91	26:28	117
6:1–6	91	26:30	117
7	106	**Romans**	
7:58–60	64	1:16–17	9
8:5–6	95	2:1–5	65
8:12	107	3:23	25
8:26–40	90	8	44
8:35–36	107	8:1–11	43
10:9	18	8:14–17	43
12	106	10:16	107
12:21–23	111	10:17	33
14:8–18	117	14:10	65
14:15	107	15:14–15	9
17	96, 100–101	**1 Corinthians**	
17:16	100	3:16–17	9
17:16–34	96–98	11:26	33
21:33	117	12:13	94
22:4	106	13:5	99
23:21	103	15	106
24	103, 105	15:1–8	106
24:5–6	104	15:23	35
24:12	104	15:25–26	33
24:14–15	103	15:50	42
24:21	104	15:51–57	33
24:22	104	**2 Corinthians**	
24:23	105	1:4	13
24:24	x, 104–105	3:2	12
24:24–25	107	4:5	25
24:25	105–108	4:6	11
24:26	105, 108	5:9–11	106
24:27	105, 117	5:10	65
25:10–11	117	5:17	12
25:13	117	**Galatians**	
25:13–22	117	2:14	107
25:13–26:32	109	2:20	26

3:8   ix
3:26–27   87
3:28   6, 94
5:13–26   44
Ephesians
2:14–22   9
4:4–6   86
Philippians
1:21–30   106
1:27   107
2:1–11   79
3:8–11   35
Colossians
2:9   35
3:12   79
3:17   107
2 Thessalonians
1:5–12   65
1:8   107
1 Timothy
2:4   71, 93
3:8–13   91
Titus
2:11–15   107
2:12   107
Hebrews
2:1–4   32
4:14–16   79
11:1   32
James
1:27   5
4:13–17   108
1 Peter
1:3–12   32
4:11a   107
4:17   107
2 Peter
3:9   26
1 John
1:8   26
1:9   13
3:2   35
3:4–6   67

2 John
9   107
Jude
3   107
Revelation
20:11–15   65

CONTRIBUTORS

Bill Bagents (DMin Amridge University) is Professor of Ministry, Counseling and Biblical Studies at Heritage Christian University, Florence, Alabama, USA.

Jeremy Barrier (PhD Brite Divinity School, Texas Christian University) is Professor of Biblical Literature at Heritage Christian University, Florence, Alabama, USA.

Ismael Berlanga (DMin Lincoln Christian University) serves as an Army Chaplain Clinician Resident at Walter Reed National Military Medical Center in Bethesda, Maryland. He is also the author of *Imperative: Studies from the Book of James*. Ismael and Brigette have been married for 15 years and have two children. Ismael has a passion for teaching and preaching. Before transitioning to Active Duty, he served at the Second and Wallace Church of Christ in San Saba, Texas.

Nathan Daily (PhD Claremont) is Vice President of Academic Affairs at Heritage Christian University, Florence, Alabama, USA.

Ed Gallagher (PhD Hebrew Union College) is Professor of Christian Scripture at Heritage Christian University, Florence, Alabama, USA.

Justin Guin (MDiv Freed-Hardeman University) is Adjunct Instructor at Heritage Christian University, Florence, Alabama, USA. He has served the Double Springs Church of Christ (Double Spring, Alabama) as the youth/associate minister since 2004.

Wayne Kilpatrick (MAR Harding School of Theology) is emeritus professor of church history at Heritage Chrisitan University, Florence, Alabama, USA.

Todd Johnston (MMin Heritage Christian University) serves as Executive Director for the Tennessee Children's Home—West Campus in Pinson, Tennessee, USA.

Robert Mann (MDiv Heritage Christian University) is the Pulpit Minister for the Park Avenue Church of Christ, Titusville, Florida, USA.

Tim Martin (PhD Amridge University) is the Education Minister for the Mt. Juliet Church of Christ, Mt. Juliet, Tennessee, USA.

Zack Martin (pursuing PhD at Midwestern Baptist Theological Seminary) is the pulpit minister for Cedar Springs Church of Christ, Louisville, Kentucky. USA.

Joshua Pappas (MMin Heritage Christian University) is Preaching Minister at LaVergne Church of Christ, LaVergne, Tennessee, USA.

Andrew Phillips (PhD Regent University) is an Adjunct Instructor at Heritage Christian University, Florence, Alabama, USA. He has preached for the Graymere Church of Christ in Columbia, TN since 2011.

Thomas Tidwell (MA Heritage Christian University) is an elder and preacher at the South Cobb church of Christ, and the Director of the Marietta Campus of Georgia School of Preaching and Biblical Studies in Marietta, Georgia, USA.

Baron Vander Maas (MA Harding School of Theology) is the Minister at Mt. Zion Church of Christ, Florence, Alabama, USA.

CREDITS

BEREAN STUDY SERIES

God Battling for the Heart of His People (2025) Forthcoming

Encountering the Gospel (2024)

Led by God's Spirit: A Practical Study of Galatians 5:22–26 (2023)

Majesty and Mercy: God Through the Eyes of Isaiah (2022)

For the Glory of God: Christ and the Church in Ephesians (2021)

Cloud of Witnesses: Ancient Stories of Faith (2020)

Visions of Grace (2019)

Instructions for Living: The Ten Commandments (2018)

Clothed in Christ: A How-to Guide (2017)

What Does Real Christianity Look Like? A Study of the Parables (2016)

The Ekklesia of Christ: Becoming the People of God (2015)

COMING IN 2025

The theme for the 2025 Berean Study Series is:
God Battling for the Heart of His People

CYPRESS PUBLICATIONS ONESIMUS BIBLE STUDY SERIES

Joy and Comfort: Favorite Psalms (forthcoming 2026)

Confident of Your Obedience: Favorite Sermon on the Mount Texts (forthcoming 2025)

Refreshing the Saint: Favorite New Testament Texts (forthcoming 2024)

Love of the Faith: Favorite New Testament Texts (2023)

To see full catalog of Heritage Christian University Press
and its imprint Cypress Publications, visit
www.hcu.edu/publications

Milton Keynes UK
Ingram Content Group UK Ltd.
UKHW011135010424
440421UK00001B/28

9 781956 811551